The Cause

The Power of Digital Storytelling for Social Good

By Tatiana Garrett Mulry
Founder of edRover.com

Copyright 2013 by Tatiana Garrett Mulry

Published by DDx Media, Inc., Creators of the Award-winning Fundraising Platform, edRover.com

25876 The Old Road, #65
Stevenson Ranch, CA 91381
DDx-Media.com

ISBN-13: 978-0615782157 (DDx Media, Inc.)
ISBN-10:0615782159

Feedback? Questions!
Visit TheCauseBook.com to get in touch.

Help Us Spread the Word!

If you like the mission and the content of this book, please take a moment to review us on Amazon.com. The more feedback we get, the more we can improve and help more amazing cause leaders tell their incredible stories of impact. While you are at Amazon.com, please share "The Cause" book on your favorite social network.

Free Bonus Resources:

To thank you for all that you do to make the world a better place, we've placed bonus resources at our website.

Visit TheCauseBook.com or scan this code with a QR Code reader on your phone:

Tatiana Garrett Mulry

Table of Contents

Tatiana Garrett Mulry

Dedication

To my three boys, who gave up lots of help with homework, trips to the park and mom's homemade cooking while I dedicated my attention to this book and our ventures. I love you Tom, Will & Aidan. You are the best gifts that I could ever hope to give to this world, and I'm so proud of the young men you are becoming.

To my husband, Will who has followed me to the ends of the earth and back. I love that you and I balance each other, laugh together, finish each other's sentences and want to be together always. You are a great dad, friend a wonderful husband and an inspirational non-profit and business leader who has taught me and so many others a great deal about living a life of selfless service.

To my parents, Judy Garrett and Paul Garrett, for never, ever letting me know there might be limits to what I could accomplish. To my brothers and sisters, nieces and over-abundant crop of nephews and Godsons for their boundless love and support. Family is what life is all about, and I'm blessed to be both a Garrett and a Mulry.

Every coach needs a coach, and I am in debt to my business coach Julie Zuzek for helping me believe in my mission again and use all the resources I had to go for it. You are amazing at helping others see their amazingness.

To my team who believes in our mission to help our clients make a bigger impact on the world through digital media, I appreciate all of your support and patience. When I look back at how much we have accomplished in such a short time, I'm full of wonder, pride and admiration for your talents. Special thanks go out to Lori Peterson and Etienne Botha who have stuck with me through thick and thin, (I mean really, really thin) and never let me give up on my dream to spark a social good movement through technology.

To my clients, who choose to work with me because they know how much I care about them, and about making the world a better place. I really appreciate that you put your trust in me and feel the same sense of commitment to social good and giving back that I do. In fact, I wouldn't have it any other way. I'm so proud to work with people who are some of the finest human beings, volunteers and generous donors on the planet.

To my very special friends, who each shared something amazing with me this year, I treasure your gifts, inspiration and friendship: Carrie, Ally, Sally, Melissa, Nancy, Pam and Tally.

To all of you who choose the road less traveled in your quest to make the world a better place, I hope the pavement I've laid down for you here will make your journey a bit smoother and more rewarding.

Introduction

While sitting on my rickety, wooden stool, waiting for someone who would want to buy my first cup of lemonade, I was sure that I would make a tremendous difference in the world. Even at age 8.

You see, I had taken a double sized piece of construction paper and decorated it with bubble letters with colorful markers that soaked into the page, "Kids for Kids – Lemonade 15 cents". My plan was to sell a bunch of lemonade, pack up the nickels and dimes and ship them to Africa where I knew things were much worse than in my suburban New York neighborhood.

In my own apartment, my stay at home mom took care of me and my four younger siblings, while my dad brought home a Seminary librarian's salary. Our clothes were all lovingly hand sewn by my mother and I remember opening games as Christmas gifts from the Penny Pinchers Thrift Store with worn boxes and missing pieces. We were far from well off, but still I wanted to give.

Having the heart to give, didn't mean I would immediately be successful at fundraising though. My lemonade stand was doomed to failure. Come dusk, I was called inside with my full pitcher, my cups, my makeshift stand and my sign. Not a single nickel or dime rattled in my collection box. You see, I lived in an apartment building at the dead end of the top of a huge hill and no one came close to my stand that day. I wish someone had told me, "Location, location, location."

I would persist without much success – attempting to sell daffodils for the American Cancer Society in the spring and Girl Scout cookies during Lent (when everyone at a Seminary gives up things like sweets and spending money on junk they don't need). I would try to fill up Read-a-Thon pledge forms, but my extended family was scattered to all corners of the world and my neighbors were already hit up by the more aggressive and popular fundraising kids who lived at the bottom of the hill closer to the center of campus.

Since I was so miserable about failing at fundraising, I let destructive ideas into my head like "Money is the root of all evil." In my 8-year old wisdom, I convinced myself that if I could only become president and could abolish money, everything could be fixed. It didn't seem fair that some people have too much money and others go without basic human necessities.

My relationship to money and my ability to pitch effectively to people with money didn't improve for many years.

Fast forwarding to high school, my now single mother of five told me the night before I took the PSATs that if I didn't get a perfect score, I was not going to be able to go to college because I wouldn't get a scholarship. No pressure, right? I stayed up all night wondering and worrying about how I would go anyway. It turned out that I was a dynamite test taker, especially under pressure, made the National Honor Society, aced my SATs and using four college application waivers provided by my high school, got into four excellent colleges.

Money was still a major stressor though, and I went to the school that gave me the best financial package – a full tuition scholarship, with student loans to cover almost all of my room and board. I watched my mother get physically sick with worry all summer since we still had to come up with $900 that first semester.

After my 1st semester in college, I never accepted another penny from my mom despite her bottomless well of willingness to give. My insane work ethic kicked in, and I worked a solid 30 hours a week while taking the maximum course load so that I could finish in three years instead of 4 and save a year's expenses. My mom continued to struggle heroically, as she miraculously sent all 5 of her children through 4-year college degrees on an assistant's salary and little or no support.

10

Since college, I've had a successful 20-year career in financial services and digital marketing helping dozens of Fortune 500 clients get their brands noticed. I've also managed to balance a wonderful home life. I've been married for 17 years and have three active boys in two schools, 2 scouting units, and a crazy number of sports and church activities.

Chasing an entrepreneurial bug led me to ask my expanding family to move 4 times in 5 years, from Connecticut to California. In 2010, I left my posh, secure corporate life behind for a crazy, risky, exhilarating life of a social entrepreneur.

While it is not easy to navigate, I love working in a field that lets me balance my parenting and volunteering with serving higher purpose and working with clients that I love and admire. Now I work with business owners, non-profit leaders and social entrepreneurs to drastically increase their visibility, their lead generation and their sales using digital storytelling and remarkable tools.

Luckily, you are holding 20+ years of my professional experience marketing some of the biggest brands and some of the humblest but most noble start-ups in the world. I've worked with huge budgets and tiny budgets, with people who are great speakers and advocates for their brand and others who have no clue about marketing or technology, but who need to grow their impact and influence.

I hope that the lessons of "The Cause" help you to shine in your community, magnetically attracting volunteers, donors, investors and partners to grow your mission and achieve your boldest goals.

Are You a Joiner Too?

I have a confession to make. I'm a serial joiner, active in many High School activities including our school's first girls' soccer team, Chorus, Forensics, AFS, and was our church's youth group president. I volunteered at a Special Olympics sports camp as a soccer coach for a week every summer and when I got to college continued to volunteer for Best Buddies, for various New York City charities as a member of our President's Club, and started a religious club on campus. Once I graduated, I served as regional director for a church youth group, and a Sunday School teacher. Now my volunteer commitments are Sunday School superintendent, Cub Scout Den Leader, classroom volunteer, and choir member as well as supporting countless other galas, golf outings, and other charity events. Whew!

Yes, some of us are joiners, givers and volunteers, and if you are reading this and nodding, I know you are one too. Like me, you've probably suffered your share of disappointing fundraisers, painful planning meetings, and elated successes.

We are a unique tribe! We care deeply about social justice, doing the right thing, helping others, making the world a better place, and we want everyone else to be just like us.

The trouble is, most people are not like us. During our rapid series of moves, I had a pause from volunteering and had time to reflect on what was important to me. Before jumping back into PTAs, Scouts, and extracurricular activities, I wanted to take stock, observe how things worked and study some of the challenges that volunteers were facing. The issues they faced weren't unique or surprising. They were nearly universal:

- A handful of volunteers did all the work, while the majority of others stood around and soaked up the benefits

- These volunteers became more and more bitter, and found it hard to hide their frustrations

- The outsiders felt more and more alienated and attacked

- Those who could barely spare any time felt guilty and tried to make up for the time gap by throwing money at the problem

- The money throwers never got properly thanked and became bitter as well

- The cycle of bitterness, passive aggressive rage and guilt money swirled around with patches of gossip

- Some brave soul tried to hold it all together until they could no longer take it and resigned

- The power vacuum swallowed up the next victim leader who would try to revive the organization and start again

This was just a dramatization, of course, but I will swear on my frayed copy of Roberts Rules of Order that there were traces of this drama in every single place we lived, in every organization we supported. And I would venture a guess that they exist in your favorite organization as well.

When the economy tanked in 2008, we had just moved to California, like so many others, I had lost my job when the venture capitalists pulled the plug at the start-up, and the social good community was hit hard. All of the organizations we belonged to were struggling due to budget cuts, plummeting donations, and personal financial terror among donors who were losing their homes, their cars, and their jobs in record numbers.

The past few years have been absolutely devastating to many schools and charities and we are just starting to see a pulse in the donation flow as the economy creeps back to life.

For the record, I don't believe in politics, bickering and overanalyzing. I believe in service, generosity and personal responsibility. Therefore, there will be no more finger pointing, blaming, or negativity as we continue on this journey together. I'm not here to debate policy or take sides. I just want to serve you all in getting your messages out into the world. Do we have a deal?

Also, for the record, I put my life savings where my mouth is. Because I found myself complaining and whining too often about severe fundraising dysfunction and volunteer burnout, I built and launched a platform for school fundraising called edRover.com that I believe solves a lot of the issues with traditional fundraising. If you are interested in exploring new fundraising opportunities for your non-profit, I encourage you to check it out.

In the past few years, I've dived even deeper into the non-profit world, having been asked to sit on several non-profit boards (which I politely decline because I love helping many non-profits, not just one, and being on a Board requires extreme long-term, loyalty and dedication to a specific cause), working with schools and charities through edRover.com, being a member of a local alliance of non-profit leaders and serving as a pitching coach for the Los Angeles Social Venture Partners. Through these activities, I've been exposed to countless opportunities to hear schools and charities talk about their fundraising struggles, and fumble their appeals for donations.

However, when a non-profit leader can powerfully embody, express and share the mission, vision, impact and financial case for support for their non-profit, I've also seen them be showered with love, support and funds. The digital tools of social media, websites, blogs, mobile apps, email newsletters and more become a giant megaphone for their cause. It is a beautiful thing to watch.

I realized that one-on-one coaching and campaign management was not reaching enough people – there is never enough time to sit down with everyone who asks for my help, although I desperately want to help, so I decided to write this book as a first step to help many more people make a tremendous impact. I hope that "The Cause" is a powerful gift for you and your organization.

Please share your questions, comments and success stories with me at Facebook.com/TheCauseBook or Twitter.com/TheCauseBook. I do read every comment and hope you will take advantage of the wonderful community that is growing around this book.

Chapter 1: Fighting Fundraising Fatigue

I know God will not give me anything I can't handle.
I just wish that He didn't trust me so much.
Mother Teresa

Here comes the tough love. If I don't call it like I see it, you won't recognize the problem and you certainly can't fix it. But if you stare into the guts of your organization's checkbook, and look at the declining results of your last few years' fundraisers, you know in your heart that I speak the truth.

Your supporters are overwhelmed, exhausted and disgusted. Your pleas for support, the endless photocopied flyers, the newsletter articles, the announcements, the invitations to events, the pledge forms and order forms are going straight into the recycle bin with the desperate appeals from the other nine organizations with which your typical supporter has ever developed a connection. It is all white noise and no one cares as much as you do. You sense that is true, right?

The family that stores the cookie dough, frozen pizzas, wrapping paper, cookies, nuts and popcorn from traditional product fundraisers wants their garage back. The Box Tops chairperson is sick and tired of spending hours and hours ripping off expired shards of boxes, weighing, bundling and mailing boxes only to get a few hundred bucks. Relatives are sick of buying overpriced, cheaply made, slowly shipped, ugly, fattening junk. They don't want it or need it. Yet 80% of Americans purchase from these fundraisers every year because we don't want to seem cheap, mean or out of touch with social issues.

Sleazy Fundraisers are Dead

Sleazy product sales fundraisers don't move or inspire us. They just numb us. We crave something more meaningful.

People are looking for straight, honest talk about what an organization truly needs to make a tangible impact, followed by a simple, passionate, heartfelt request for support. They are willing to help in many ways, but they need the requests to be more organized and coordinated, and the volunteer tasks should be easy to perform during downtime with the tools they have on hand.

They want to be asked to use their skills and talents to help the organization and to be recognized publicly for their contributions.

They want you to be compassionate and understanding about their other pressing time commitments like the J.O.B. or business that pays them enough to be able to write a big old check whenever you ask.

Here's some perspective: during the back to school month, my three children brought home 25 separate fundraising requests from school, scouts, sports and church, not to mention the direct mail and dinner time solicitation calls we get from a dozen or so charities.

I'm often confused by the mixed messages that are sent. Organizations that promote a healthy lifestyle and conservation are exploiting our kids by selling unhealthy products, with wasteful packaging and manipulative sales techniques that trick people into buying things people don't need to support a good cause.

Truth be told, most product based fundraisers only return about 20-40% of the proceeds back to the organization. All of this work, storage, financial management (or worse – mismanagement), logistics, volunteer hours, delivery hassles and more are taking their toll on volunteers and the people who love them.

How long will our friends and family tolerate our incessant requests to support organizations that don't directly benefit them, whose missions are not well explained and whose products are not needed?

Many supporters don't understand the fundraising mechanisms, or are so disconnected from the "machine" that runs the organization that they don't feel their efforts are needed or appreciated so they don't bother to investigate. Many feel like they have never been asked to do anything personally.

What makes any of these organizations think they are winning us over with this kaleidoscope of distraction, confusion, bulk, paperwork and calories?

In many non-profit organizations, core donors are getting worn out from constant requests to make fundraising goals just to keep the basic functions of organizations alive.

As long term supporters of a non-profit, particularly in hard economic times, it can be difficult to keep a connection to the original hope and the vision of the organization. When the board members or core donors are the ones that feel completely responsible for the welfare of the organization, they are looking internally and fretting about the future of the organization.

I would argue that this model of relying on a core few donors to bail out an organization constantly is actually a symptom of a lack of vision, planning and outward inspiration that will be necessary to compete in a more connected world. It doesn't need to be this way!

Old School vs. New School

"Old school" fundraising is broken, and "new school" fundraising is just getting started. The case for leveraging digital storytelling and new tools for donor engagement and fundraising is strong.

We live in an extremely connected society, one in which there are cell phones than there are people (in the US) and where we spend several hours a day engaged on our computers, phones and TVs with connected content. As a society, we are used to navigating our worlds with maps and directions on our devices, shopping online, getting entertained, informed and inspired through connected media.

The problem is that the non-profit sector is not keeping up with the trend. Facing severe budget cuts from government-funded programs and shrinking household budgets of core supporters, many non-profits have decided to double and triple down on the old fashioned, inefficient ways of raising money. Online giving grew 11% in 2012 vs. 2011, but still only accounted for 7% of all charitable giving according to Blackbaud's The Charitable Giving Report.

The Problem Won't be Solved by Technology Alone

We have to collectively get better at an age old craft that has been handed down generation to generation. We have to master the art of human connection through effective storytelling.

It is my wish that you will use this book to reinvigorate your growth and communication plans to build a broader base of fund development sources for your organization.

You will be able to get core donors and new donors of all sizes excited by the renewed vision, mission and digital communication plan you will be able to build using this book, they will be relieved and excited about continuing their support for your organization.

Action Steps

1. In a notebook or on your phone or computer, start making notes. Start with this: "I give myself permission to think differently, do things differently and connect with our supporters differently."

2. Identify 3-5 people who pop into your head when you think of the tired, complaining, grumpy donors or volunteers that you sick of coddling but are afraid of losing. Make a pledge not to focus on them for a while. They will still be there after you give yourself the space to define your modern fundraising strategy.

3. Identify 3-5 people who pop into your head as curious but quiet observers of your organization that you'd like to get to know. Write them down and keep them in your head while

you read this book. They are the people you will be focused on reaching and inspiring.

4. Put a moratorium on new fundraisers unless they WOW and captivate your followers, require little effort and have tremendously high yield.

5.   Make a promise to yourself to work through at least one chapter a day until you complete this book. Write down your promise.

Chapter 2: Working on Your Own Mindset

When your work speaks for itself, don't interrupt.
Henry J. Kaiser, US industrialist

What are the obstacles to fundraising success? Most of them are mental – figments of the dark and stormy version of our imagination that consumes us when we dwell in the negative.

Remember my screwed up relationship with money? It caused me to give and invest in social good programs without considering their performance rationally, and then questioning anyone who didn't give or seem to care. This was massively screwing up my chances of making an authentic, personal, respectful appeal to other potential donors or investors. If they didn't care, I didn't want their money. My bad attitude about money was getting in the way of expanding my mission and helping more schools and charities, big time.

Oddly, when I worked in the for profit sector, I was an acclaimed expert at communicating passionately about the brands I worked for, measuring every click, optimizing the messages and tools, and driving for results.

If we are in a poor money or success mindset, it is like there is this negative beast in our imaginations chanting ominously whenever we attempt to take action:

- I'm not good enough

- I don't know enough and I'm afraid of looking silly

- I'm afraid of looking like a phony

- I'm afraid of my organization growing out of my control

- I am too new

- I am too old, too young, too fat, too skinny, too ugly, too pretty, too dumb, too nerdy to be taken seriously.

- No one wants to hear my message or buy what I'm selling (I actually stood up at a conference and confessed that one last year – wow)

- I'm afraid that if this doesn't work out soon, I'll have to go get a real job, so I don't want to get too attached now

- My programs are not ready, are unworthy or are not up to snuff

- I'm asking for too much money

- I'm afraid they will say no

It is time to stop that bickering right now. I know for a fact that none of those excuses are true. If they were, your organization would not be where it is today, and you wouldn't be the one standing at the helm. You were uniquely designed for this job, given the talent, passion and patience to forge ahead and make a tremendous difference in the lives of the population you serve. There is something in your story that pulled you forcefully into this role, and that is the spark that we must uncover in order to help you tell a compelling story to inspire and adhere others to your mission. It is all in your outlook and attitude. It is all up to you.

Many times founders of organizations are the most severely afflicted. They lack the perspective and support that comes from sitting in a more junior role in the organization. They feel their identity is so completely consumed by the organization that they can't step outside of their story to think about it and represent it objectively. So often founders get swept up in the day-to-day drama and delivery of their organizations mission that they never step out of their business to work ON their business strategy and therein lies the challenge. Their business will never grow without them connecting to the outside world for support, validation, customers and media attention.

Many founders that I've worked with are perfectly content to continue their mission as "mushrooms" – in the dark and covered with dirt (among other choice materials). This book is to encourage founders and other leaders to emerge from the shadows and shine a light on the good work being done and ask for support to add fuel to the fire of the mission.

The goal in the early stages of an organization is to experiment with different approaches with the hope of finding a formula that achieves the most positive outcomes for the least amount of funds and effort. Once that formula has been discovered, it is time to take action to find the resources required to turn the formula into a sustainable business.

This is the point at which many fine leaders want to get the heck out of there. The crippling self-doubt kicks in.

- What if I can't find someone reliable to help me?

- How can I do more than I'm already doing?

- What if "they" want us to change things?

- What if "they" start examining us and criticizing us?

- What if things don't get done the way I wanted them to get done?

- What if quality suffers?

First of all, you don't even know who "they" are…these people who may or may not care enough about your mission to get involved financially or as volunteers. Until you know whom you are dealing with, you can't waste energy on this. What if "they" are the coolest, most supportive people on earth who introduce you to resources beyond your wildest imagination and multiply the impact of your organization by ten or even twenty fold? Do you still resent them before even meeting them and getting to know them?

Second of all, it would be almost impossible to find someone who cares as much as you do or will work as hard as you work to get the job done, but you can only do so much. Soon, you will need help and they will introduce new variables, good and bad. They may work slower, more deliberately, need to ask more questions, find gaps in your processes, make suggestions, and maybe, in all of that analysis, they find ways to make things better, to take care of details you no longer have time to consider, and to give you the time and space to define and pursue a more exciting vision for your organization.

When you are reaching out for supporters or staff, you must do so from a place of utter generosity. This is a time when you need to portray 100% alignment with your mission, give 100% of your passion, and exert extra energy and time. You need to show how committed you are, to paint a picture of the future you are envisioning and to convince supporters and staff that their unique contributions of time, talents and funds will make an enormous difference in the outcomes you are trying to achieve. To get them to join you on your mission, you must be the living embodiment of your mission.

You must be able to tell your personal story of connection every time you interact with supporters and staff. You must be willing to get raw and vulnerable, to share the dark parts of yourself that embarrass you or frighten you but that connect you to your passion for impact. You must share why you have chosen to serve others in this way so that people can connect to you, get energized, understand what is required, how they can help and persuade them to take action.

People Hear Autobiographically

The key to communicating with supporters is to realize that they experience your story *as if it is happening to them*. They must connect to your vulnerability and your experience based on something they see in themselves. People who will take action to help your cause don't just sympathize with your story, you must help them empathize through your words, images, body language, behaviors and actions.

- What is your big WHY?

- Have you been in the shoes of your clients and have you successfully transformed your life in a way that serves as a model for others?

- Can you point to an important person or event in your life that thrusted you in the direction of this type of service?

- Are you doing this for your own good as well as the community around you, so that you can point out that we are all in this together?

Woe to Win Story

Telling your story of woe to win takes courage, emotional strength and generosity of spirit, but it will trigger a powerful, visceral response in everyone who hears it.

What is woe to win? Think of a backwards country song. Instead of starting out with everything and losing the girl, the car, the horse, the buddy, flip it on its head. Build trust with your audience by describing the lowest point in your life or in your star client's life and building up the little successes until you reveal the big win.

I have worked with a non-profit pitching contest as a coach and witnessed the power of this transformation. When contestants shift from reporting the facts to becoming passionate, personally engaged advocates for the mission and describing the massive impact a small donation can have, the room just goes bananas. We are all yanked by the collar and pulled into the story because we see ourselves in the struggles that are being addressed by the organization.

Don't settle for rattling off facts when you can personally engage the audience with your personal story of commitment to the mission and outcomes of your organization.

Once your audience members are each individually connected to your story, you must be clear about your expectations for the relationship – what do you need from them, how much will they be expected to do, and how confident you are about their capabilities.

Even if you connect with them through your story, but they you set low expectations for their ability to give or volunteer, you insult them and dampen their enthusiasm. When your body language and voice hint that you don't believe they will give, they sense that you are right. Your conviction is not there, and therefore, their conviction vanishes as well.

Money is Never the Real Issue

Have you noticed that people find money to buy things they really want? Or to donate when they are really compelled? Or to throw all of their effort into a volunteer position if money is tight? People will find a way to be a part of this success story if you make a compelling, personal appeal.

Don't apologize for being awesome, committed, vibrant and alive because you are fired up about the mission. Don't shy away from describing what your organization needs to thrive because you are worried about how it will be perceived.

Speak the Truth

Find creative, honest and simple ways to express your joy, hope and enthusiasm and you will not be ignored. Share your confidence that you can lead your "tribe" to the positive outcomes of your vision and you will possess the power to transform lives – not only of your clients, but also the lives of the donors and volunteers who participate along the way.

People want to follow leaders who choose to lead. They want to be inspired to bold action, urged to greatness and they want to be acknowledged, valued and cherished along the way.

Action Steps

1. Define your big WHY.

2. Outline your story of "woe to win".

3. Rehearse with a friend or family member.

4. Go out and practice.

5. Find a coach or a speaking group.

6. Keep practicing.

Chapter 3: Strategic Planning

The best time to plant an oak tree was twenty-five years ago.
The second best time is today.
James Carville

When you start to plan your organization goals, a process that should take place at least annually, it can be difficult to maintain an objective perspective. If you are always immersed in the daily fires, finding and setting aside time to contemplate, think, get inspired and create goals is nearly impossible to imagine, let alone do.

I beg you, for your sanity and the health of the organization, to take at least a day, if not two or three, away from the office or command central to plan.

Make sure that you are prepared to review a SWOT analysis of your organization with your board, at least annually. This stands for Strengths, Weaknesses, Opportunities and Threats – it is usually presented in a grid of 2 boxes by 2 boxes, with SW on the top and OT on the bottom.

- Your Strengths are things you know your organization is good at and should continue to exploit for growth.

- Your Weaknesses are areas where you need help, in the form of additional resources, new skills or increased focus to help your organization.

- Your Opportunities may be programs, education, donor engagement, grants, contests, or marketing techniques that you feel should be evaluated and possibly pursued for the benefit of the organization.

- Your Threats are factors that could chip away at your organization including competition, alternative solutions, staffing, financial, environmental, economic or regulatory issues.

Furthermore, your plan should review all of the basic elements of your organization, and set goals for the future year, three years and five years.

1.   Strategy & planning

2.   Marketing

3.   Development/Sales

4.   Operations

5.   Financials

6.   Staff & Professional Development

7.   Legal/Regulatory/Tax

Every member of your board should be intimately familiar with the plan, and especially the financial results. They should all have their fingerprints on the strategic planning activities and be held accountable for reaching the agreed goals.

From this point, you will have a roadmap for everyone in your organization to follow, and a yardstick to measure success. It is incredibly important for your board members to possess this information so that they can make appropriate decisions and drive progress. In a small organization, this may seem like a lot of work, but it is absolutely essential for proper management.

There are many excellent books on strategic planning. If you need a recommendation, please comment on TheCauseBook.com and we'll help you out.

Now it is time to rekindle the enthusiasm of your team, your clients, your donors and volunteers about your plan.

Action Steps

1. Take the time to type out a strategic plan for your business, if you haven't already, or grab the one you already have done and keep it by your side while you work through this book. Make notes in the margins or in your new plan about ideas you'd like to incorporate.

2. Schedule time to meet with other non-profit leaders in a "mastermind" group at least 1-2 times a month. Talk about things that are working for you, ask for help on things that are not working for you. If you need help pulling together a group, contact us and we'll help you find peers – just reach out on TheCauseBook.com.

3. Take the time to do online research about key regulatory and economic issues and connect to your federal, state and local government officials on Facebook or Twitter to stay informed and have a direct voice in the discussions on issues.

4. It is time to be creative about marketing, staff development and programming ideas, In your notebook, brainstorm at least 10 wild and crazy ideas without editing yourself. See what comes up – the revelations may surprise you and give you great ideas for sparking life into your plan!

5. Your development and sales plan will undergo a big transformation as we work through the rest of this book. Be ready to make changes to your plan as you have "eureka" ideas or investigate new solutions you had never considered.

6. Get your board on board and have them contribute their ideas, talents and skills to beef up your plan.

Tatiana Garrett Mulry

Chapter 4: Your Key Audiences

The size of your audience doesn't matter.
What's important is that your audience is listening.
Randy Pausch, Carnegie Mellon Commencement Speech, 2008

In any organization, there are a few masters to serve and juggling all of their interests can be a full time job – considering the need of your customers, suppliers, employees, landlords, investors, the media and others is a complicated business.

In non-profit organizations, the most important of the audiences you serve are your beneficiaries or clients and your donors. Think of your donors and volunteers as your "investors". They may not want a strictly financial return, but they do want to know that their hard earned funds are working hard for the outcomes your organization has promised.

Get to Know Your Clients

Let's consider the point of view of your beneficiaries/clients first. You may assume that you know what they need because you have been serving them for a while. But have you really asked what they need lately? Perhaps things have shifted for them based on economic factors, employment opportunities, personal growth or circumstances, the impact of your previous services, the presence of other organizations that serve the same population or other factors outside of your control.

The best way to handle this needs assessment is a survey and/or follow up interviews with your clients. Ideally, you should be doing this annually as a part of your planning process so that you can adjust your programming to suit the ever-changing needs of your client population.

Here are some general questions to ask them. Please adapt your own set of questions to meet your specific organizational needs:

- How satisfied are you with each of the services you are providing? (Scale of 1-10)

- Would you recommend our services to a friend or family member? (Yes/No – if yes, provide name and contact information)

- Are there any services that you need that you are not able to get from your organization or any other organization in the area? (Yes/No, If yes, describe)

- Are there any staff members or volunteers that you would like to recognize? (Please name and describe)

- Are the prices reasonable for the services we provide? (If you charge for services – Yes, No, If no, please explain)

- Are the benefits you are receiving in line with the effort you are exerting to help the program (Ask if there is a volunteer requirement of your beneficiaries – Benefits exceed effort, benefits equal effort, effort exceeds benefits)

- Do you plan to continue to use our services in the future? (Indicate expected length of service requirement: 1 month, 3 months, 6 months, 12 months, more than a year)

- What outcomes have you observed this year? (Describe – this question should be tailored to the specific outcomes your organization measures)

Asking questions similar to these should help you uncover critical needs in your service population, help you predict service volume requirements, recognize and plan for staff, and help you tweak existing programs while setting a course for designing new programs that will be needed in the future.

From this baseline understanding, you can begin to chart a course of action to deliver your programs cost-effectively and efficiently. There is no reason to provide services that are not valued, and there may be reason to create new services as your client population changes. Do you have the proper staff and volunteers to deliver the programs your clients need? Do you see ways that your program can be expanded to serve more people with existing staff or service formulas? Are there natural partners that you should approach to fill in service gaps and expand your impact?

Repeating this survey annually will help you measure progress from year to year and continuously optimize your delivery. This is critically important step because increasingly donations are directly correlated to proving that your organization delivers positive, cost-effective outcomes.

Gathering testimonials and success stories is also incredibly important. Ask your clients to sign a release for use of their photos or videos in testimonials. At a minimum, grab your cell phone video camera and film your clients answering a few simple questions:

- What was your situation before coming to our organization?

- How did you find us?

- What services have you utilized from us?

- What results have you experienced?

- Why would you recommend us to others?

Having 5-10 of these simple videos on your website and published to multiple social media sites will help your organization with visibility and credibility with donors and will provide you with more referrals quickly.

Make a goal of sharing one of these stories in each monthly newsletter you distribute and create a montage of the videos for use at events where you are looking for donations.

Now that you have a few of these stories, you can put them into the hands of an army of online messengers and ask them to pass along the inspiration. Put the images, videos and words in their hands for easy sharing and specifically tell them to like, share, repost, pin, tweet, etc. to help your organization. Each post should have a link back to your donation page to make it easy for new and old supporters alike to take immediate action.

Donor Centric Models of Engagement

Since the 1960s when Robert & Jean Blum made the concept popular, the charitable sector has looked at donor engagement in a simple pyramid model with a broad base of small donations at the bottom and planned legacy gifts at the pinnacle of the pyramid.

In 2008, Tony Elischer, managing director of the voluntary sector consultancy THINK Consulting Solutions, made the case for adding more layers and nuances to the pyramid to allow for the variations in entry points to the fundraising pyramid introduced in the digital age.

So often we think of our mission as development officers as moving the donor from level to level like a chess piece. But in reality, a donor can't be manipulated that easily. They must feel embraced by your organization, valued for their contributions of any size and fully linked and committed to the long term vision and strategy in order to make more sizable gifts.

Often, even the smallest donation is made under incredible scrutiny. We all have immediate access to charity watchdog reports, Internet reviews and ratings on any charity, and many of us have been trained to be cynical about giving. Could it be that the 19 telemarketing solicitation calls a week in the month of December, the mountains of direct mail and the incessant requests to attend galas and events, and the urgent pleas to buy over priced products are getting to us and making us wonder if the money is going to anything meaningful at all?

The linear stage step model is too stifling for current fundraising atmosphere. Many are now advocating for measuring engagement and ability to influence in a "vortex" shape with continuous flow and no ultimate pinnacle like the pyramid.

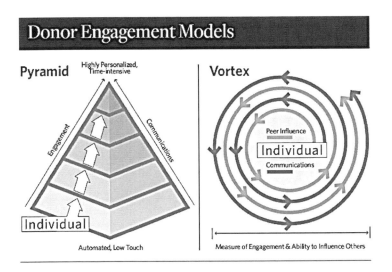

Image Source: http://www.ssireview.org/articles/entry/the_permanent_disruption_of_social_media

Today, we are immersed in messages from traditional and social media. Donors become aware of multiple worthy organizations from many sources and may become involved through any of the touch points. Gaining their loyalty, trust, commitment and financial support may require a shift from traditional approaches – as eco-conscious, privacy conscious donors are repelled by wasteful mailings and intrusive phone calls.

There is also work to capture their affection and convert it into active advocacy to their friends, family and business associates through word-of-mouth and online discussions. Some may want to advocate publicly and some may choose to be active by working or donating privately. They may choose to increase or decrease their support at any time, so you need a personal, direct, one-to-one connection with each donor to understand their needs and motivations to keep giving them the fuel to keep their passion and commitment alive. With this personal method of donor cultivation, there is no fixed end goal, just a unique approach to cultivating each donor.

This changes how staff is trained and how donors are engaged over time. Let's explore this in more detail, shall we?

The Value of an Influencer

A person who donates a little, but influences 100s to donate may be just as valuable if not more valuable than someone who quietly supports at a generous level of financial commitment.

In the past, lifetime value calculations only took into account average donations, future capacity to donate, attrition rates. Now we also need to look at the person's following, a measure of their influence (like Klout.com), their propensity to share, and their effectiveness at sharing.

Treat Your Donors as Investors

Donors have plenty of places to spend their money. According to the Association of Fund-raising Distributors and Suppliers, schools and non-profit organizations raise over $1.7 billion each year by selling popular consumer items and 80% of Americans support these programs.

Approximately 10% of GDP in the US can be attributed to the non-profit sector, with donations to religious institution in the lead. [1] Corporations and foundations account for 16.5 percent of total dollars given (U.S. Census Bureau 2002).

From this, it is clear that there is quite a lot of money that can be claimed by the organizations that make a compelling case for support. Can you answer why donors should support your

---

1 Christopher Eaton Gunn Third-sector Development: Making Up for the Market (Cornell University Press, 2004) 0801488818, 9780801488818 Partially Accessible Copy on Google Books (accessed July 6, 2009 on Google Book Search)

organization in a way that opens the faucet of charitable funds or social investment?

Why Do People Give?

It is important to understand individual donors', foundations, grantors and other supporters' motivations for giving. The cynical and obvious answer is "tax deduction". Large organizations and wealthy donors are certainly aware of the tax advantages of charitable giving. But that does fully not explain why 90% of Americans give to charity every year.

The fact is that 73% of U.S. adults say being involved in social change is personally important to them. People are more likely to join and share social change discussions online than to start them. Four out of five adults believe that they can make the world a better place by their actions. Ok, who is that grumpy fifth person anyway? Sounds like somebody needs an attitude adjustment!

Most of our lives we spend trying to maximize our resources, yet we see so many people taking joy in giving away part of their income. It seems like the ultimate paradox.

Intuitively, we know that giving is part of our basic human need to find meaning in life. We feel connected to our family, to our community, to our faith, to issues that have impacted our lives and at some point, we start to feel the compulsion to contribute in ways that are personally meaningful to us. Once our basic human needs are met, such as food, sleep, security, we turn our attention to a deeper meaning according to Maslow's Hierarchy of Needs.

Maslow describes self-actualizing people [2]:

- They embrace the facts and realities of the world rather than denying or avoiding them (including self-awareness).

- They are spontaneous both in their ideas and actions.

---

[2] http://www.ssireview.org/blog/entry/why_do_people_give_to_charity/

- They are creative.

- They are interested in solving problems; this often includes the problems of others. Solving these problems is often a key focus in their lives.

- They feel closeness to other people, and appreciate life.

- They have a system or a framework of morality that is fully internalized and independent of external authority.

- They have discernment and are able to view all things in an objective manner.

But with so many choices out there, how does someone make a decision to financially support a specific organization or respond to a particular appeal?

Let's go a little deeper in the research on this subject:

- Giving is very sensitive to permanent changes in income while consumption remains fairly steady.

- While neither gender or marital status is more generous than the other, research shows that men will be more generous than women when it is cheap to give, while women will be more generous than men when it is expensive to give. 3

- Donors presented with a matching opportunity tend to be more generous by 20-100%.

- Donors are focused on outcomes that stretch the impact of their dollars for demonstrated good…as examples:

    o Organization A informs potential donors that $17 can immunize a child against the six major childhood diseases and $40 can provide large wool blankets to

---

3 http://www.pitt.edu/~vester/whydopeoplegive.pdf

protect ten children from the cold/winter weather during an emergency

o   Organization B states that $35 will buy two high-energy meals a day to two hundred children and $100 can pay for infection-fighting antibiotics to treat nearly forty wounded children

- Donors give because of social expectations and they tend to give as much as they think others should give.

- We tend to follow the leader. Seeing a peer donating or increasing their level of donation tends to provide an incentive to step up donations by a smaller amount. That's why events and auctions are so powerful.

- Repeated interaction is important for continuity of donation. Most givers are accustomed to supporting the same charity year after year or month after month and will continue to do so if the results of the donation are positive

- Many donors want to build a legacy or a reputation for generosity in the community and crave acknowledgement even if they are not asking for it explicitly.

- Many feel guilty for not having a direct positive contribution to society through their work. They are craving fulfillment that they are not getting from their jobs. That is not to say that their work doesn't help society, but that they don't feel the personal connection and satisfaction of working directly with clients to make their lives better.

As a former banker (I like to say a "reformed banker") who worked on internal technology projects, I remember feeling disconnected from the end customer and yearned for work where I could see the direct correlation of my efforts to positive outcomes. Do you know any people who are striving to find more meaning in their work? They are great prospects.

The way you engage supporters for major gifts may be different than trying to establish a broader base of smaller funders. Assuming that major gifts are either being handled well by your organization, or seem elusive given your size and short history as a non-profit, we are focusing on strategies for going building a broad base.

Donors make funding decisions on an emotional level – because you and your cause touched their heart. The rational factors support that emotional decision. You must be able to connect on both levels through your storytelling in person and through digital media to increase your effectiveness.

The Top 10 Things Potential Supporters Crave

Each donor is searching for a number of answers to important questions before jumping on board with a financial donation, volunteer position or board position.

1. *Personal connection* – Is the mission something that a donor truly connects to and identifies with. People are drawn to different causes for different reasons, but normally, they must have a personal connection to feel compelled to assist the organization.

2. *Programs and Proof of Outcomes* – Does the approach to solving the problem make sense? Is the program the right tool and right scope to handle the problem? Is there sufficient evidence that the programs are helping to drive positive outcomes for the service community? Are there numbers and testimonials from clients who have been through the program?

3. *Path and Plan for Sustainability* - Is the program scalable or transferrable to other geographic areas or subjects? Can the program add beneficiaries while scaling costs at a lower rate? Will program revenue cover costs at some foreseeable date so that the fundraising burden can be reduced or eliminated? If not now, when?

4.   *Accountability* – Does the staff seem competent and trustworthy? Is the board active on policy, fundraising, staffing and oversight?

5.   *Transparent communication and finances* – Does the organization talk openly about issues and share their filings as required by the IRS? Do they have good ratings with CharityNavigator.com?

6.   *Relationship with money* – Will this gift be the best use of my money? Will the organization use my money wisely and amplify its impact? Are there other pressing financial matters that I should attend to before making this gift?

7.   *Talents and Interests* – Am I going to be able to contribute more than just money? Do I have talents, interests, skills or experience that will be valued by the organization? Will I develop new skills or experiences

8.   *Relationships* - Will I deepen current relationships or develop valuable relationships by being involved? Is someone I know, admire or love leading this organization?

9.   *Legacy* – Does this fit with my own picture of the legacy I want to leave? Is this something I want to be associated with? Will I be comfortable standing up for this organization, saying I contributed and asking others for support?

10. *Acknowledgement* – Will this bring me the recognition and appreciation that I'm craving in my life (whether or not we admit this, it is a big factor). Would it feel good to be recognized publicly for my good works and accomplishments with this organization?

Action Steps

1.   Create and run a survey to get feedback from your clients. (Try SurveyMonkey.com)

2.   Create and run a survey to get feedback from your clients.

3. Based on these responses, identify candidates for testimonials.

4. Book a half-day with a videographer and invite your clients and donors to share their stories.

5. Write down five changes you will make to the way you engage with donors, clients and prospects given the material you just read.

Chapter 5: Packaging Your Requests for Support

The only really good place to buy lumber is at a store where the lumber has already been cut and attached together in the form of furniture, finished, and put inside boxes.
Dave Barry

Recognizing all of these needs, it is important to segment the packages that you will present to your potential supporters into different levels. Always stress that packages are flexible and can be tailored to an individual, corporate or foundation donor's needs.

Your proposal should tell your story in a compelling way with a summary of the highlights and sponsor benefits on the first page, an engaging case study that clearly illustrates the impact your organization has, your mission, your program(s) description, the organization background, key staff and board bios, and financial responsibility stats. A great statistic that predicts or describes the efficiency and sustainability of your organization can be very compelling as well – "with a gift of just $152 a month, we can feed an entire family, teach them how to shop for healthy, nutritious and economical foods and then pass along their new skills to another family".

Include the following sections in the "ask" section of your proposal:

- A clever name for each of your levels

- Level of support or investment

- Clear and compelling benefits to the sponsor/donor – exposure, product sampling, recognition?

- Deliverables – what outcomes or services will be delivered for the money invested

- A list of other well-known past and present supporters – foundations, corporations, celebrities or donors for credibility

Now the trick is to ask them for support! Once you have it, you can put them to work and acknowledge the wonderful blessing they have provided.

If you have found them on social media, definitely thank them publicly there! This is part of building community and tapping into an incredible peer network. Once people see someone they know being thanked, they will definitely check your organization out.

If they have given as an event, auction or in a private meeting, ask how they would like to be recognized.

Action Steps

1. Your request for support or sponsorship is one of the most important things you need to prepare for your organization. Many leaders of fledgling non-profits believe they are not ready to ask, but you need to be prepared and try to really find out if that is true. Start by committing to have at least 3 informal meetings or phone calls with friendly potential sponsors to discuss their expectations and needs when they support or sponsor an organization.

2. Incorporate what you have heard from the sponsors into a proposal containing these sections:

   - Overview of your organization and summary of benefits to the sponsor

   - Case study illustrating the impact of your organization

   - Background and history of the organization and leadership

- Sponsorship package levels with a clever name, investment level and an escalating list of benefits to the sponsor and deliverables for each level

- List of current and former sponsors

- Call for action and contact information

Chapter 6: Selling – Let's Get Comfortable

Although prepared for martyrdom, I preferred that it be postponed.
Sir Winston Churchill

In non-profit circles, we do a lot of soft selling…we squirm around that word when we make an annual appeal, ask for pledges, beat around the bush in the hopes that donors will come out of the wood work to help with our mission. In reality though, we need to be asking directly for the help that we can prove will push the outcomes we all want in society.

What if all the sales people and development people in the world went away suddenly? What would happen to our economy and social services? Everything would immediately grind to a screeching, devastating halt! Yet sales people are often thought of with disdain. Many of us don't want to be perceived as being inauthentic or sleazy. We need a total mindset revolution on this point if we want our organizations to be successful.

Selling is not evil. Think of selling as service – in the case of non-profits, you are putting donors' funds to work to produce incredible results in your community, which will benefit not only your clients, but also the society at large.

Answer 2 Questions

Is your organization doing great work?

Is this work worthy of recognition and support by the community?

If you answered yes to both of these questions, then you are not actually selling, you are making people aware of an incredible opportunity to serve. And in transmitting this message, you yourself are providing the ultimate form of service.

If you answered no to either of these questions, then you have some more work to do to align your programs to the needs of your clients, to find a business model that provides efficient delivery of service, to make sure that you are in deep, mad, passionate love with your mission, and to make sure you have scripted a careful way of describing your vision to the world so that more supporters can be magnetized to your organization.

Notice the selling techniques in every large organization's direct mailing pieces. Why do they use tear-jerking stories, photos of clients, passionate pleas for support and promises of rosy futures? They have all hired incredibly talented direct sales copywriters to craft the perfect written pitch. Of course, you know you've responded to one of these pieces before. They are good, really good. Start saving samples in a file so you can emulate and adapt those great ideas.

Can you produce the same results for your organization? Does this intimidate you at all? It's ok…we all get intimidated by this piece. It is not simple to get your story right, or to understand exactly what will resonate with the right donors. Even the best copywriters on earth use a little bit of instinct and a lot of testing to get it perfect, and it is not a job that is ever fully complete. Our culture and economy are constantly changing, prompting new ideas to be required to maintain the effectiveness of any appeal.

So, the real question is, do you truly believe that your product, service or cause produces benefits to society? If so, it is time to craft and deliver your service story.

After all, my wise and inspirational friend, Ferlie Almonte, says that N.O. just stands for "New Opportunity". Just be thankful for the lessons learned and feedback from that conversation and look forward to the next time when you will get to tell your story more powerfully, and effectively. You have shared your story and planted a seed for sewing in the future with the people you spoke with or others they know.

Sharing, Selling's Pretty Cousin

Some say beware of the "Slackivists", people who are willing to share on social networks but not much else. However, studies have shown that they donate as much as anyone else, are twice as likely to volunteer or participate in a walk, and are more than three times likely to solicit donations.

People who are comfortable sharing your message are going to amplify your communication power beyond anything your organization could have hoped.

Ask your supporters to share, and provide materials they can use easily on:

- Email
- Facebook
- Twitter
- LinkedIn
- Instagram
- Pinterest
- Tumblr
- StumbleUpon
- Digg
- Reddit

What can you ask online supporters to do?

You may have your doubts about getting real support from online connections who have never met you, don't have a way of physically seeing and interacting with your organization on the ground. How dedicated can they be? What kind of influence can they have?

You may be surprised at the number of easy, low friction tasks you can ask your online tribe to do to support the cause:

- Buying products that support the cause

- Donating personal items

- Signing a petition

- Attending an event or book tickets

- Learning more about the issue at an event or workshop

- Forwarding an email

    These tasks begin to dive into the area of influencing others:

- Joining a cause related group on a social network

- Posting a logo for the cause on Facebook and asking others to do so

- Wearing the cause logo on clothing or jewelry

- These tasks require more personal involvement:

- Volunteering time

- Sponsoring someone financially

- Donating money

- Taking an active role at an event

- Contacting political representatives

- Donating services

  These tasks require both personal involvement and have the potential to influence others to positive action:

- Blogging about the issues or cause

- Inviting others to join the cause group on social media

- Sending personal emails about the cause to contacts

- Talking to contacts about the cause

- Requesting that others take actions like contacting political representatives

- Recruiting others to sign a petition

- Organizing an event

- Requesting donations for the cause

  The key to making this work is to offer great content and ask people to speak from the heart, and on a regular basis. Authenticity, consistency and personal commitment are required to spark real influence for your cause online.

> **Bonus Tip:** Be strategic about what you ask someone to do for your organization. Make sure it is rooted in a deep understanding of the cause and a commitment to serve.

Action Steps

1. You are going to need to practice telling your story of impact and letting people know how much money your organization needs. Yes, it is a big number. Yes, your organization serves so many who deserve the support. Yes, it is worth it. Yes, people will be happy to contribute when they hear your passion and envision the outcomes that can be driven by their contribution.

2. Also practice asking for support at different levels. You need to be as comfortable asking for hundreds of thousands of dollars from large philanthropists as you are asking for five dollars from someone you meet at the grocery store.

3. Brainstorm and write down a list of 20-30 small but specific, any time things you want and need supporters to do. These are great to have on hand to sprinkle into all of your communications. Write a few blog articles about the items. Post one a day to Twitter. Create a handout for networking events. Keep each idea in a jar on your desk when someone comes in or calls offering to help, pull out an idea and put them to work!

4. Find five places to share your organization's story this month.

    *   Offer to write an article for your local magazine, newspaper or Chamber of Commerce newsletter.

    *   Offer to give a speech at a networking or civic group meeting.

    *   Write to your local radio or TV station to let them know you'd like to share five tips for helping the cause.

    *   Send an update or note to your legislators about your organization and the progress you are making. Share your opinion on an issue that impacts your clients.

    *   Share your story with a random stranger at a party or waiting in line for the movie theater.

    *   Absorb the feedback and the wonderful feeling you get from telling this incredible story! It will be fuel to fire you up about asking for one more very important thing.

    *   Ask for the money. It is not a shame and it is not a crime. It is an investment in your community's future and in your organization's long-term survival. Once you have told a moving story, state your organization's total level of need and ask if they would be willing to help with a contribution.

Chapter 7: Personally Enrolling Supporters

And so, my fellow Americans: ask not what your country can do for you - ask what you can do for your country. My fellow citizens of the world: ask not what America will do for you, but what together we can do for the freedom of man.
John F. Kennedy

The art of personally enrolling donors and volunteers is extremely valuable for any non-profit leader. Everyone in your organization should be a highly committed, well-trained, fluent, comfortable and authentic ambassador for your organization. But that doesn't happen automatically. Every person needs to travel along a learning curve and a yearning curve. They must be encouraged, trained and motivated to want to do their best for the organization.

Bringing passive bystanders into the fold by acknowledging and assigning their talents is the number one way to increase success in your organization. Those who are paying attention, always attending, but not raising their hands are just waiting to be valued and approached with a suggestion. Ignore them or scorn them at your own peril. Not everyone dives in with both feet. Some need to test the waters to make sure there are no sharks. Be a lovely, gentle, friendly dolphin and invite them to play.

Social media makes this even easier. In just a few minutes, you can spot which supporters like or share your content consistently. Reach out to those people personally (online, but even better by phone or in person) and give them an important job of serving as your digital ambassadors, spreading your key messages, videos and images online.

Enrollment Case Study – Recently, I met with a brilliant, passionate and lovely MBA student with a heart for the giving arts. She has so many potential career options ahead of her, working in a for-profit company advocating for social good, working in a company that focuses on media for social change, and serving as a board member on a small non-profit that serves underprivileged youth with sports training and college counseling. It is a great organization that I also support.

I asked her if she was involved in the sport fostered by the non-profit she assists and she shook her head no. How strange! Most people would be attracted to that organization based on their affinity for the sport and the great outcomes they achieved. Clearly she was still very passionate about this wonderful organization. So, I asked her how she got involved.

One day she was walking in her neighborhood and bumped into her long time school friend's mom who had just started a non-profit. The non-profit leader praised the young student for her knowledge and let her know how much her skills and experience as a business student could help the non-profit. Would she like to get involved in a prestigious board liaison position? Of course, the student eagerly agreed because she felt honored by the request, eager to contribute and was happy to be seen for her merits.

The non-profit got dedicated service from a smart, passionate, helpful, student who had been masterfully enrolled by a savvy non-profit leader.

Have you experience being enrolled masterfully? The volunteer position you couldn't turn down or the donation you felt compelled to make?

Can you do the same thing with up and coming leaders in your community?

Action Steps

1. By now you must have a few ideas about what the skill, experience and passion gaps are in your organization. Write down those gaps in your notebook.

2. Next to each gap, write down three names of people that you know or a brief description of the person you are looking for that could fill the gap.

3. Make appointments to meet with the people you know this week and let them know how much their specific talents could help your organization grow. Ask them for their support!

4. For the gaps you are not able to fill by enrolling people you know, talk about the gaps and qualifications you seek with several people this week. How many? Depends on the gaps, and the people you talk to! Commit to a number that feels right for you by writing it in your notebook.

5. Don't have a clue or a contact that can help you find these skills? Do a search by skill and location on LinkedIn, or draft and post an irresistible Craigslist ad for help.

Tatiana Garrett Mulry

Chapter 8: Combatting Burnout

The only tired I was, was tired of giving in.
Rosa Parks
(on refusing to give up her seat on the bus)

Often times, non-profit leaders grow to resent the casual observers, the uncommitted, and the bystanders who hang out on the fringes of the organization. The assumption is that they will never commit, will never step up, and will never take a leadership role. The current leaders don't understand their hesitation and mistake it for laziness, lack of interest and even nastier - spitefulness or jealousy.

I would argue that this is more of a sign of respect on the part of the sideline observers for the leaders. They see you doing everything and not asking for help, and they think their offering to contribute will be seen as meddling.

You may be calling me nasty names right now and don't believe my wacko interpretation of the situation, but I've seen it again and again. These people are just waiting to be seen for their talents and asked to play a meaningful role. They obviously care about the organization or they would not be standing there as observers. Let that soak in for a while.

They also represent respite care for the weary leaders! So how can you turn this situation around, embrace the observers, and create a larger, more vibrant and engaged group of volunteers and donors?

Here's a 7-step plan for turning a low-energy organization around:

1. *Listen* - Ask lots of questions at your meetings – calling on even the quietest observers and engage them in the discussion.

2. *Investigate*- Find out about the unspoken worries and objections that don't come up at your meetings, but fester in gossip swamps between the meetings. Don't think people will just tell you what they think. They don't want to bother you. You seem too busy.

3. *Spotlight* - Discover the hidden talents of each member of your organization. People want to be seen and recognized, so introduce new people to the group highlighting their talents, interests and commitments.

4. *Relate* - Form more relationships with group members. Make it a point to talk to 2-3 different people for 5 minutes before and after your events or meetings. Don't just gravitate to your close friends and colleagues.

5. *Empower* - Set clear expectations for 100% involvement. Provide specific responsibilities and donation plans for everyone in the organization, even people who don't raise their hands. Ask them personally for their support.

6. *Measure* – Hold people to the benchmarks and results they sign up to meet. Accountability is really important to people, even in a non-profit setting. No, I take that back, especially in a non-profit setting! This is an area where you can really set your self apart from other groups that are not holding people accountable for their commitments.

7. *Celebrate* - Make sure celebration and gratitude are #1 on your agenda for each meeting and event. Start and end by thanking contributors and celebrating successes.

Action Steps

1. You, my friend, are about to start a movement. Take a deep breath, and brace yourself for the adventure of a lifetime. This is your moment of truth.

2. In your notebook, write down how you will introduce your own version of our 7-step plan at your next meeting.

3. Your future communications can also follow the 7-step plan. Think about having sections of your newsletter or website dedicated to each of these steps. Write down any inspirations you have about communicating with the 7-step plan.

Chapter 9: Telling Your Service Story

Technology adds nothing to art. Two thousand years ago, I could tell you a story, and at any point during the story I could stop, and ask, Now do you want the hero to be kidnapped, or not? But that would, of course, have ruined the story. Part of the experience of being entertained is sitting back and plugging into someone else's vision.

Penn Jillette

Your story of personal connection and service to your cause is a rare and wonderful gift you can give to inspire others to join the effort. Making a personal case for involvement helps people to connect on a deep, empathetic level with your service.

At their core, most people would never start a non-profit or a social good company, would not step up to lead, would barely craft the narrative of their own personal story, or lead a life dedicated to service, unless they are inspired by YOU to do so.

This is my personal mission and I invite you to make it yours too. To inspire others to truly live, give and serve by telling THEIR story.

It is important that you map out your story in stages, just like a Hollywood movie. It has to have an arc with a stage setting beginning, climactic middle and satisfying ending.

One tip to building a great story is to start backwards. What is the big finish that will surprise and delight the audience. It should be focused on the amazing outcomes you have witnessed during your service to the cause and share your emotions about the impact you have seen. From there, think of an intriguing way to introduce your story. Describe the characters involved and the dilemmas they face. Amplify the problem, by twisting the metaphorical knife, to help everyone truly feel the depth of the issue. When it seems all hope is lost, you are ready to introduce your powerful ending.

With this approach, you can paint a vivid picture of the positive human impact your organization makes.

The biggest mistake that fundraisers make is to focus on the objects you would like to purchase with the funds you are requesting. People don't donate for smartboards or computers, they donate to inspire imagination and hope for a better future for students. Describe their joy in discovery, make the story "physical" – the teacher tapping the smartboard and exploring ancient ruins that make history come alive for students on the edge of their seats.

One night, on a rare date at the movie theater, after buying our tickets, the attendant asked my husband and I if we wanted "to support a child in need" tonight. Now I realize that this kind of Point of Sale request for support has historically been very effective, and that retail staff is often trained and required to make these requests. However, they have gotten so frequent and so generic that they don't mean anything anymore. Even I (a person who finds it hard to say no to any request for support), had to say, "What need? Which child? What outcome? Which organization? What is this really about?" There was no signage, no trusted logos, no explanation for such a bland request. Yuck.

Please don't fall into this lazy trap. If you are going to enlist retail partners for your mission, they must be able to passionately describe your specific mission and outcomes even you can only get them to share one sentence. "Give a hungry child the hope of a hot meal tonight with your gift of just $5" or "Help a needy child get life-transforming facial surgery with your gift of $100" would be much more inspirational and deserving of support than "support a child in need".

People want to see, feel, hear and touch the tangible results of the gifts they give. It is your mission to help the audience you serve, but you are also delivering fulfillment and redemption to all of the donors and volunteers you enroll.

It is all in the simple packaging of your mission and outcomes.

Action Steps

1. You are about to close your eyes and think of a time when you felt really uncomfortable, scared, out of alignment, wronged, hurt, angry and your antidote was to feel committed to doing good work in the world. Close those eyes, really dwell on the memory and only open them when you are ready to jot down a full description of that moment!

2. How did you get enrolled in supporting this cause? Was it a mentor or a friend asking you? A catastrophic event that caused you to seek it out? An accident? No, there are no accidents – you said yes for a reason. Write it down.

3. Write down a powerful, juicy, emotional sentence that describes why you are passionate about your organization.

4. Roll all of these answers together into a short paragraph about why you feel it is important to serve, how you got involved and why you are so passionate about the organization.

5. Practice this frequently and then roll this speech into your discussions with supporters new and old.

Tatiana Garrett Mulry

Chapter 10: Crafting The Perfect Pitch

Anything's possible if you've got enough nerve.
J.K. Rowling

I promise you this: you are only one pitch, one video, or one memorable photo away from achieving the goals you want. Everything you say, and every gesture you make must be deliberately crafted and expertly and effortlessly delivered in a way that is designed to make them curious and intrigued to take the next step.

You must change your tone. Stop the begging and supplicating. Stop the twiddling your hair and shuffling your feet. Stop hiding behind podiums.

You are driving good people away with your misplaced assumption that your organization doesn't deserve support and that you are probably going to get a no. Don't start every conversation by apologizing for doing great work for a worthy cause.

Let the cause and impact speak for you. You are just telling an incredible story of impact, your own personal transformation and then invite others to transform their lives by being a part of this incredible movement.

Your messaging must be consistent, confident, powerful, creative, and on "brand". Your organization's brand is embodiment of the way you want to be seen. It should be beautiful, pulled together in a pleasing, dynamic design, and held together by strong, dynamic, impactful words that linger in the memories of each person you engage.

Do you believe in your mission? Does your message reflect that strong belief? Really, there is no sense in going on with the recommended exercises from here if you don't feel that what you are doing is of utmost importance and deserving of respect. Take the time to dwell on this point for a little while if you are having trouble swallowing this. You are dedicating your life to this mission. It better be worth it!

Now that you believe in your message, you must believe in your heart that you are the very best messenger to deliver this story and invitation. Your audience is there because they want to hear what they have to say. They are being incredibly generous with their time and attention, so recognize them for this right away. Show that you know that they care deeply about this issue and that they've proven this by their attention and attendance. You appreciate their talents and what they collectively can do to amplify the impact of the mission.

Stand in your own power, don't fidget or shuffle – you are an incredible engine of transformation and hope for your cause. The key to delivery is to be your self. They want to know why you do this incredible job that seems so hard and self-sacrificing. Share why you put in the time, let them get a glimpse of your passion, share your purpose. Let them know you expect some of them feel the same way and want to know how they can help. Share with them the types of talents and donations you need to achieve the next level of impact. Tell them you know many will want to help, but won't take the initiative if they don't know how they will be valued. Make a promise of value and recognition for donors. Make a promise of satisfying work that will leverage their talents to the fullest. Make them a promise that their commitment will have meaning.

When you make "the ask", share the benefits they will receive:

- Personal satisfaction

- Rewards and gifts appropriate for each level

- Recognition

In sales, a few of the most effective conversion tools are urgency and scarcity. Provide bonuses for acting quickly and/or limited opportunities for special access, tours, trips, gifts or experiences for early committers.

It takes some practice to get your powerful, committed, electric story out and make the transition to ask for a similar level of passion and commitment from your audience. I recommend that you work with a mentor, coach, family member or friend to really rehearse and hone the pitch until you feel the electricity of it radiating out of every pore. Get it on film, watch yourself, refine the speech, do it again, over and over.

1. Your goal should be to get a dynamic, impassioned, well-reasoned, factual but impactful three minute pitch video that you can put on your website, share on social media, include in your media kit and sponsorship proposals, as well as submit with grant applications, contests and other opportunities to gain support.

2. I can't wait to see your videos. Please upload them to YouTube and share the link with me on Twitter.com/TheCauseBook.

3. In your keywords of your videos, please add TheCauseBook so that all of our videos appear together in search.

4. Remember, and write in your notebook, "I am the right messenger for this job!"

Chapter 10: Dealing With No

Worry often gives a small thing a great shadow.
Swedish Proverb

There are so many organizations peddling stuff these days. My boys happen to be in the tribe that sells a popular snack food, and we have a ton of friends whose girls sell very delicious, but diet-nuking snack foods. Every year, we have an awkward avoidance and sheepish sales dance with friends, neighbors, door-to-door sales kids, grocery store blockades and now incredibly precise surgical strikes through social media, video and email requesting us to buy products.

One of the most disturbing "NOs" my middle son, accompanied by dad, endured came from a neighborhood man who answered the door in the nude. My son was stunned, but made his pitch anyway. The guy quipped that it was not a good time. Um, yes, sir, maybe after you throw on a pair of shorts? I'm afraid that experience has scarred him for life. Many organizations are discouraging or outright banning door-to-door fundraising for a very good reason.

In my house, I'm of the belief that we don't need extra over-priced snack products. We generally try to avoid them in the house. We are desperately trying to eat healthier and go to the gym regularly. Why on earth would we want to buy 8 boxes of cookies or popcorn in a single month from every single one of our friends, let alone strangers at the supermarket?

Now, I'm typically a big softie when it comes to children doing a great job with fundraising requests. My rule has been that I will buy from kids I know that make a good attempt to ask me personally – look me in the eye, explain the products, explain how the money will be beneficial to their organization.

However, one year, I was bombarded by at least a dozen dear, sweet friends' requests on behalf of their children in a single launch day – the most orchestrated launch strike I had ever witnessed. That evening, a young scout approached me at another scouting event and I completely barked at her that she was the 13th person to hit me up today! So uncool of me, and I felt bad, and of course my guilt bought me a couple of make-up boxes of cookies.

Even cause-minded people are frustrated by over-saturated fundraising campaigns. This incident made me realize that as an industry operating out of fear of lack of funds, and we are training people to ignore our traditional, repetitive, expensive fundraising appeals. I learned this the hard way – by "boothing" myself.

Outside suburban grocery store, a year later, I stood in my leader uniform with my den of 7-year old scouts for 8 total hours over 2 weekends selling our overpriced snacks. These are some of the cutest, most well behaved, well-mannered kids on earth, and they were lucky if 5 out of 100 people they asked said yes to their sales pitches. Most of the "yes" people claimed to have kids who had gone through scouting. Offering a less expensive or time-consuming way to help sometimes converted a "no" into a "yes", but it was not easy. We sometimes sold single packs of the product for a lower price, or convinced people to make a smaller cash donation. When the "no" people would actually make eye contact and chat with the boys, they had several common excuses:

- I don't have the money

- I already bought from someone else (usually commenting that you people are everywhere!)

- I have health issues that prevent me from eating this/using this product (don't get me started on the list of ailments that were described in vivid detail)

Mostly though, people ignored the boys and the cause they were promoting.

Children are born with boundless optimism and fearlessness. Putting them in a situation where they constantly hear "no" can be very frustrating to them and to parents. Dealing with rejection is a character building exercise, and it is something we all have to deal with as fundraisers. If you haven't come to grips with this yet, it is time to go out on a selling field trip with some scouts to build up that resistance.

People are absolutely bombarded by countless requests for support. Just in the first month of school last year, I collected fundraising request forms from my three son's two schools- at least 25 requests for funds, fundraising products or fundraising dinners out in a month. That doesn't count any of their other activities or the causes we personally support as a family. That ignores the telemarketing calls, the direct mail packages (thanks for all those address labels, but really, isn't this getting too expensive?), and the appeals from charities and business associates in our local community.

We have to be careful to not burn through all of our favors in the community with requests that abuse their funds. No one wants to buy overpriced stuff they don't need. Look for ways to help people contribute with direct donations that will be used well, or for ways that they can contribute while spending on things they already buy.

I challenge you to stop contributing to this never-ending fundraising noise, and focus on getting your core impact message out. Then share 1-3 simple ways your audience can support you financially or through volunteer work.

I would love to see kids standing in front of grocery stores sharing how scouting, their school or other organization has impacted their lives in a positive way and how a $5 or $10 donation would make a tremendous impact. Who wouldn't feel more connected to the cause with this approach and be more compelled to consider making a donation?

I was speaking to a young scout named Olivia, right before publishing The Cause, who is a very successful, dedicated Cookie salesperson and she reminded me of myself at her age. Her mom was

73

telling me that she and a friend hatched a plan to make and sell special barrettes in the park because the school really needed money. For all of its faults, I do think that our product sales fundraising techniques are raising a generation of kids who are determined to use their business skills to make a positive difference in the world. Thank you for reminding me of the positives ways each person can help, Olivia! You will be a tremendous social entrepreneur someday.

This fundraising fatigue was my main motivation to create the edRover.com shopping for charity platform. I wanted to provide my fellow human beings with an easy way to support their favorite school or charity simply by buying instant eGiftcards or merchandise from top brands from their mobile phone, tablet or PC. By providing a simple platform where people can make everyday purchases to support their favorite school, we hope to make a big impact on education.

Action Items:

1. Learn more and start raising funds for your organization at edRover.com.

2. If you would like to learn more about licensing edRover for non-education fundraising, please contact us at ed@edRover.com.

Chapter 11: Developing a Solid Social Media Strategy

Do not do to others what angers you if done to you by others.
Socrates

Did you know that 3 out of 5 non-profits surveyed in 2013 by Vertical Response reported spending more time on social media than in the past? If your organization isn't on board with Social Media, chances are strong that you will be left in the dust by those charities that are getting better and better at it. I'd like to make sure your organization is one of those socially savvy charities. However, I'd also like to make sure you are not just making noise and asking for money, but that you are being strategic about sharing content that matters. Your purpose in social media should be to inspire, educate, engage and build a loyal following that will ultimately support your organization financially.

One of the most exciting things about social media is the opportunity to multiply your message to the many people your supporters know. When one of your supporters is fired up about giving a testimonial about your organization, sharing a photo, video, link or event, you are getting a personal recommendation to many of the people they know.

Let's say you enlist 10 loyal supporters (perhaps these are already people you know like your board, staff and key volunteers, for example) and train them to be effective brand ambassadors. They make a pact to share content that you share, to comment on your posts and to promote your key initiatives and events online to their social media contacts.

For the sake of easy math, let's also assume that you've selected supporters with considerable influence – at least 1,000 followers.

Every time each one of them posts something, about 100 people will see it (or about 10% of their contacts and connections). That means 1000 people see each message you put out due to the efforts of the 10 ambassadors – even before you have 1000 followers on social networks.

Each time one of their supporters interacts with it, it exposes you to their supporters and makes the post more visible for a longer period of time for the original ambassador's supporters. Soon, many thousands of people are being exposed to your message.

If your message is bland, boring and begging for money, you are not likely to get anyone on board. But if it is exciting, inspirational, enlightening, surprising and eye-catching, it may take fire.

Case Study: Invisible Children

A 30-minute documentary video produced by Invisible Children absolutely scorched through the internet during the Spring of 2012 bringing awareness, donations and vocal response to address the LRA, the Lord's Resistance Army, a terrorist organization in Central Africa responsible for the continent's longest running armed conflict. The campaign promised to make Ugandan warlord Joseph Kony famous, not to glorify him but to "raise support for his arrest and set a precedent for international justice.

Their Kony 2012 series of videos has racked up more than 100,000,000 views on YouTube alone, not to mention the sharing that has occurred on other sites, and even more awareness generated through posters, buttons and T-Shirt sales.

Funds were collected using:

- Donations through the YouTube Nonprofit Program

- StayClassy.org

- A donation page on their own website

- Product sales on their website

Such an astounding success on the awareness front did bring out many critics who complained about the allocation of funds to programs on the ground in Africa vs. the costs of creating and driving the "smug", "slick", "indie" awareness platform vs. administrative ratios.

Of course, no non-profit can operate without such scrutiny and every donor should investigate the organizations they support thoroughly using tools like CharityNavigator.org.

That being said, can you even imagine your cause gaining over 100,000,000 advocates ready to help, to fight, to serve, to awaken to the needs of the population you serve?

Social media awareness building takes time, effort and money for staff or an external support team to manage the effort. However, the messages that are transmitted from advocates to their contacts are perceived as more trustworthy when compared to paid advertising.

Starting a social media presence for your organization should be looked at as an important strategy to reach your organization's objectives, not as a hobby that you look at on weekends or evenings once in a while.

You will need a full plan to develop your presence, a schedule for releasing supporting content, graphics, and videos, the proper tools to distribute content and collect donations, and a way measure success factors like impressions, engagement and donations.

If you follow the steps in this section, you'll be able to tackle social media like a pro:

Step 1: Profile Your Audience

Who is your ideal donor? It's time to paint an incredibly lifelike portrait of his or her, including writing down details about all of these factors:

- Demographics – age, gender, race, marital status, presence of children in the household, education level, race, veteran status, sexual orientation, etc.

- Location – Neighborhood characteristics, home, school and work locations

- Psychographics – what does he/she think, believe, need, get concerned about

- Affinities – what groups do they identify with or belong to? (PTA, Veterans' Groups, sports, other clubs, communities, charities?)

- Household income & spending patterns

- Health status or concerns

- Daily/Weekly/Monthly behavior

- Media consumption habits, particularly social media activities

Pretend you are a detective looking for a suspect – lay out all of the clues for how to find that ideal person. Then give him or her a name that will truly personalize the communications. This is the persona you will be speaking to as you create all of your messages online or in event speeches. It is a lot easier to talk on a deeply personal wavelength to Becky Sanchez or Mark Potter than to a thousand nameless, faceless avatars out in cyberspace.

Step 2: Find this Persona Online, Study Them and Speak Their Language

Here is where it gets interesting and a bit time consuming, but I assure you it will be enlightening. I highly recommend that you do some social media research to find vibrant, active communities that are filled with thousands of people like your persona. Spend no more than a half an hour on each site to find out where people who fit your persona hang out, what they are saying, how they are sharing content and what they really respond to. You want to see the lingo, what they like, how they interact, what time they are most active. Remember, you are acting like a detective gathering facts and clues, not jumping right in and making an immediate plea for donations!

The genius of this exercise is you are also going to encounter amazing content and discussion ideas that are working across the Internet to provoke conversation and action about your topic. Copy and paste links to great articles, pictures, videos and conversations you find in a spreadsheet or document so you can go back and integrate or adapt them for your content strategy. If something inspires you and moves you to think differently, it may inspire others too! Look for things that have a ton of likes and shares on Facebook, or Retweets on Twitter, etc.

Before you get all nervous about imitating or emulating other content producers, realize you are in great company:

- "Good artists borrow, great artists steal" – Picasso

- "The only art I'll ever study is stuff I can steal from" – David Bowie

- "We have always been shameless about stealing great ideas." – Steve Jobs

- "I invented nothing new, I simply assembled the discoveries of other men behind whom there was centuries of work" – Henry Ford

Fair warning: This exercise is a little like Alice jumping into the rabbit hole. Set a timer on your phone or computer to alert you when you are 30 minutes to an hour into one of these investigations and move on to the next. Keep track of your account names and passwords so you can go back in the future, but keep it simple to start.

Here is where to look and how to connect with them:

Forums and Blogs

There are thousands of niche forums that millions of people use to discuss important ideas. If your persona is a teacher or someone concerned with the environment, do a Google search for:

- forum: keyword

- blog: keyword

Check out the first page or two of listings for group conversations you can join. Scan the conversations for popular topics, key phrases, concerns that are actively being discussed. Join the forum and answer a few questions if you feel the spirit move you or make a few helpful or constructive blog comments along the way with links back to your website.

Facebook

Assuming you are already a personal member of Facebook, use the search feature to look for references to your keyword. You should also create a page for your organization and start to develop a content strategy for it.

Like pages relating to your topic and see what other pages they recommend or follow. You will often find great quality pages this way - like those pages too if the topics are related to your topic or audience. You should also find target-rich media company's pages and follow them. For example, if your persona is a parent and you are looking to attract more parents like her, find "Parents Magazine", "Parenting", "Parent and Child", "Working Mother Magazine", blogs written by moms, other charities that focus on connecting with moms, etc.

Pause to see what strategies other organizations are utilizing on their pages. Are they posting pictures or videos? Asking questions? Sharing quotes? Describing case studies? Notice the level of engagement under each post – the numbers of comments, likes and shares will give you a sense of what is working best for them. Make notes about clever ideas you find!

You can also share other peoples' or organizations' content to get started. Sharing content from others is a great way to get noticed by people you want to connect with. Believe me, people look to develop relationships with those that are commenting, liking and sharing content on Facebook, so it can be a good way to get to know potential advocates for your organization.

While you are at it, please LIKE our page on Facebook http://facebook.com/thecausebook and introduce yourself and your page on the wall!

Twitter

If you don't have a Twitter page already, it is time to create one for your organization. Twitter has a tremendous search capability indexed by a strange looking system of "hashtags". Active Twitter users who have been initiated into this method of tagging their topics and using them for searches use a hashtag (basically this symbol # attached to a keyword or phrase like this #keyword).

Use https://twitter.com/search to find out what is happening right now about your topic or keywords. This will help you find great people and organizations to follow who are talking about your topic.

Be on the lookout for media pages, bloggers who write and share about your topic and people with a good record of "following back" meaning they follow about as many people as are following them. When you follow them, they are likely to return the favor.

Take note of how people write their tweets in your topic area. Are they conversational – asking questions, making little observations – or are they transactional – intriguing people to click on links for more information? Do they post pictures and links to videos?

When you see an account of a person who matches your persona profile, follow them. Also follow other organizations in your space. You may also click on their list of followers and follow the people who are listening to these organizations.

Start writing a few tweets a day – some sharing ideas, some sharing quotes, some sharing links to your webpage, always including one or more hashtags related to your topic. Hashtags look like this **#word** and serve an important purpose: to make content more searchable. You can add a # to any word or phrase with words stuck together to make a searchable term. You could make up any hashtag and use it to identify your organization, a conference or event, a concept or project as long as it is in this format: #organizationname or #conference2013. Research the hashtag you want to use to see if there are other conversations going on that might not fit with your topic. If there are, you may want to use a different term. Search for and use hashtags that will help your content get noticed by your target audience – maybe conferences they go to or popular Twitter conversations about your subject. Remember, when you write with hashtags, more people searching for information on your topic can find you and follow you.

Start re-tweeting other people's great content. When people see you doing this, they will most likely respond to you, thank you and give you even more exposure to their audience.

Doing these quick steps for a few minutes a day should give you a good base of quality, well-targeted supporters who will be sympathetic to your message over time.

We'd love to interact with you on Twitter as well – follow us and say hi at http://twitter.com/thecausebook.

Pinterest

Do you have a highly visual subject of interest? You must check out Pinterest.

Let's say you have a health and wellness focus to your mission. On Pinterest, you can search for and find people sharing photos, videos and articles about healthy recipes, exercise plans, health tips, natural remedies, and more. Or perhaps you hold Gala event fundraisers? Maybe pinning evening gown fashions and photos from your last event would work for attracting your audience.

If you already have some of these types of content pieces ready, you can "pin them" by adding links on Pinterest and when others discover your "pins" they can "repin" or share them.

Start a Pinterest account for your organization, and begin to create boards named with your keywords of interest by pinning lots of interesting things that relate to the topic. Pin items that you think will attract your persona and lead her to follow your organization so that over time, you can share your mission-driven messages.

Definitely study what is being shared actively on Pinterest and take notes on the brilliant ideas that you see so that you can start developing content for your website or for direct upload to Pinterest relating to your core mission.

You can follow me on Pinterest and see the many different types of boards I have put together for personal and professional reasons to get some ideas. http://pinterest.com/mrsmulry/. Having a variety of posts and interests will broaden your appeal and help you reach more people.

Search for keywords about your topic and follow others who are pinning content about that topic. Comment on any posts that you like to gain the attention of potential followers! You can also connect your contacts from Facebook, Twitter or email to build a list of friends to follow.

YouTube

Many people don't realize it, but YouTube, a Google product, is actually the second most popular search engine. Google ranges YouTube videos very highly, and people tend to like to learn by watching videos. Your organization should have a YouTube channel set up with all of your branded videos displayed. If you aren't ready with videos yet, don't worry. Eventually, you will want to spend a good deal of time and effort here because video is so popular and engaging and can be shared on nearly all other social networks.

For the purposes of this exercise, go to YouTube and search for your keywords. Subscribe to a handful of interesting organizations or people covering this topic that have a substantial number of views. These people are likely to be very influential in your topic area, and you want to be able to easily watch their videos as they come out. You may also want to watch a few videos and comment on videos you enjoy so that you start to catch the attention of YouTube channel content producers and start to grow your own subscribers.

What kinds of videos get a lot of views in your subject area? How to? Event coverage? News reports? Speeches? Make notes about this for your content plan.

Other networks to watch that have worked for my projects and my clients:

- Instagram – This popular photo sharing app now has a website too and has grown outrageously fast because it is simple and people love it. It is a great place to share photos and quote graphics. This network also uses hashtags like this #word to make content more searchable. Search for and use hashtags that will help your content get noticed.

- Tumblr – Like the love child of a blog and Twitter, Tumblr is the fastest growing social network for young people. It is super easy to use, and great for promoting causes. This network also uses hashtags like this #word to make content more searchable. Search for and use hashtags that will help your content get noticed.

- Slideshare.net – This is a gem that not enough people know about. Upload your presentations and videos from speeches, events, webinars, etc. and watch your numbers go up. You can also capture leads if you pay for a subscription.

- Quora – Go here to ask and answer questions, especially in technical fields. Lots of experts answer questions here, and if someone is asking about your field of expertise, answering them can build your credibility and incoming inquiries about your organization.

- LinkedIn – LinkedIn is also a very powerful tool. Make sure both your personal and organization profiles are up to date here and connect with everyone you meet after a networking opportunity. Share posts to LinkedIn or ask questions or give answers to amplify your visibility.

Step 3: Set Your Goals and Objectives

I hope the last step was helpful to you to understand where your people hang out and how they like to engage. It is useless to say I want a million Twitter followers by the end of the year if you don't know how to find the right million Twitter followers who will be open to taking action on behalf of your cause. One highly engaged, influential follower can and will do a lot more good for your cause than a million spammers. You should go for quality interaction and responsiveness, not quantity.

This next exercise helps you set goals for your social media efforts.

What types of things would you like to achieve with your social media plan? These could all be legitimate parts of your goals:

- Increase traffic to your website

- Improve the conversion rate for donations

- Improve the volume of donations

- Enhance donor engagement

- Grow your list – aka, your reachable audience (followers, likers, subscribers, newsletter opt-ins, etc.)

- Reduce costs relating to traditional marketing

- Improve your "green" quotient by reducing print and other wasteful forms o marketing

- Sell out a successful event

Measuring success is also important. If you are successful with your efforts, what will that look like?

- Increase of xx% in donations

- Reduction of xx% in marketing costs

- Increase your list by xx% per month

Putting specific numbers to your goals helps you to determine down the road if you are reaching your goals and tells you when you need to tweak your approach to improve.

Step 4: Create and Deliver Your Content Strategy

Now you know exactly the persona you want to attract, where they hang out, what bait they like and how to measure success. It is time to pack up your fishing gear and get ready to find some loyal supporters! I find that the easiest way to do this is to create a document or spreadsheet to get organized.

Start by taking an inventory of the main web pages you need your customers to visit in order to achieve your goals. These could be your home page of your website, your top social media pages, your email or contact management system opt-in page and a direct donation page. If you have a mobile app, and most organizations should be considering that these days with mobile phone penetration exceeding the actual population of most countries, you need to have your app links listed here too or a smart landing page that will redirect visitors to the appropriate app store based on their mobile device.

You can download our companion app for this book that has great resources from cause marketing experts by searching for "The Cause" in your phone's app store (iOS and Android) or by scanning this QR code (for any smartphone):

Scan to download: The Cause App

Go to a URL shortening service like http://bit.ly and create shortcuts for each of these website addresses. This will help you track clicks. You may also want to experiment with long addresses that have not been shortened providing people can see a descriptive title of your page. Some studies have shown a higher click through for these links vs. shortened links.

Everything, and I mean everything you produce needs to direct visitors to one of these pages. And each one of these pages should also point to another one of these pages if not all of them.

Your website and/or donation page should be featured in your profiles for your social media pages.

When someone likes you on Facebook or opts-in to your email list, you can suggest that they visit your homepage or follow you in other places too. The point of social media is to give people your message in the places they want to consume it.

Now that you have your links organized, it is time to start developing content to promote these links. First, you must decide on the Key Messages you are trying to convey as you speak about your brand.

Elevator Pitch

Do you know what an elevator pitch is? It is the speech you can blurt out in the time it takes to ride the elevator with someone in a position to fund your project. A popular term in the investment and entertainment industries, an elevator pitch is something you can use all the time to peak interest in your cause when you meet someone at a networking event, seminar or conference. The purpose of the pitch is to intrigue the audience enough to make them want to learn more about your organization, not to deliver an entire case for support in 30 seconds.

What is your "elevator pitch" – how can you best describe your organization in 30 or less seconds that will intrigue the audience to want more information?

It needs to include four critical elements:

1) What is your organization's WHY? What motivates you to do the work that you do? What is your purpose or your promise to the community you serve?

2) What problem are you trying to solve?

3)   What is your unique solution and how does it stand apart from other solutions? What specific strategies or programs do you use?

4)   What specific action do you want the listener to make? Donate, volunteer, learn more?

Everyone in your organization should have this speech memorized. It should be short, clear, easy to say, appeal both emotionally and rationally, but be fun and memorable.

Next, we need to put a little meat on the bones. What are the top 10-20 key talking points you could deliver from there to keep them engaged and digging deeper. These messages form the core of your content strategy.

Everything else you do, share or say needs to support, enhance or lead people to those messages.

> **Bonus Tip:** Think of those messages like a wonderful closet organizing system (I sure could use one of those!). Your key message/elevator pitch is your main clothing rod. Your other pods and modules are the supporting messages. Hanging your clothes, or folding an putting them away in the other sections represents filling out your content strategy with beautiful messages that all work together to present a strong case for support.

You need to make a real effort to get the tone right. Sounding super formal and corporate is a sure fire way to get some people to tune out, while for others, sounding like a surfer dude may be totally bogus. What language does your audience use when talking about your subject? Borrow that real language and highlight what people are saying. Make it relevant to what people are going through, real news stories and jump into the conversations that others are having by responding in a natural way. Most of all, relax and have fun with your audience. They want to know the people behind the cause and everyone wants to feel welcome, just as you would welcome them into you home, a meeting or an event.

Plus, your brand needs its own personality – a unique blend of ingredients that will help it stand out from all the other messages in your field. Don't be afraid to be quirky, funny, challenging or controversial if you feel that will boost your brand visibility.

The ten most powerful words in the English language for copywriters are: *You, New, Save, Health, Safety, Guarantee, Love, Discover, Results, Proven.* See if any of these words can help strengthen your pitch and talking points.

You will need to work through your content again, this time making sure you are invoking emotional triggers when you talk. These are the tried and proven triggers that make people decide to buy from advertising:

- Fear – "Don't be left out"

- Guilt – "Your contribution means the difference between life or death"

- Trust – "No hidden costs"

- Value – "You won't find a better deal/more impact"

- Belonging – "Join today and see what everyone is talking about"

- Competition – "Be the envy of your friends"

- Instant Gratification – "Your money will be put to work instantly"

- Leadership – "Be the first of your friends to step up"

- Trendsetting – "Be like these celebrities"

- Time – "The need is urgent - sign up today with our representatives"

Creating Contagious Content

Your whole purpose for developing a social media strategy should be to inspire a growing group of supporters to spread your message. This is not the viral outbreak you want to fight against! Learn the techniques that work for other organizations and put them to work for you.

As you are starting to create content, you must decide on your objective for each post. The primary purpose for any communication needs to be:

- To entertain

- To educate

- To inform

- To inspire

With these guidelines in mind, here are the different types of posts you should plan to create and share.

Sparkling Conversation Pieces

Think of these ideas as the banter you would use at a cocktail party or water cooler to get to know people. These posts introduce people to your organization, what you care about, what principles you stand for and give them the information they are craving about popular subjects relating to your topic.

- Spark a regular conversation – let people know what you are working on or looking forward to, what the weather is like, how you are feeling – be human and be real

- Make comments about pop culture – musicians, TV programs, movies, popular toys, celebrities or politicians (if you are not a political organization, be careful not to be too partisan or you may lose half your audience) are all fair game for comments and people love to talk about them. Be nice, friendly, supportive and fun, and you may attract some of those pop culture icons as supporters.

- Ask thought provoking questions – this is a real time research opportunity to gather audience feedback on important issues or key decisions. Let your supporters know that their answers will truly be considered as your organization moves forward with your service strategies.

- Share relevant news articles – post news articles relating to your topics

- Announcements – make announcements about your organization – big wins, events, new hires, new job openings or volunteer opportunities

- Lists – Create numbered lists that structure your best advice or discoveries. Start the articles with things like "Top 10 Tips for", "3 Best Tricks to", 7 Favorite Apps for", etc. People love numbered lists because they are easy to read, benefit from and share.

- Product, service, tool and application recommendations – if you love a product or service, give it a boost by commenting about it. You may find they will be thrilled to learn about your feelings and may be open to a sponsorship relationship.

- Negative statements – sad, but true – these get a lot of engagement. You don't have to go and stay negative, but once in a while, drop the Pollyanna ploy and let a real tone of disappointment fly.

- Mistakes and difficulties – people love brands that can admit and recover from mistakes gracefully. They also respond to stories of courage and bravery in the midst of difficulty.

- Fill in the Blanks – This is the "Mad Libs" approach to engagement. No one can resist commenting on the blank word in a sentence. I would walk my dog in the rain, but I'm afraid of _____. Watch the answers pour in.

- Polls and Surveys – this is a more formal version of the questions idea. Using Facebook polls or one of a number of survey tools like SurveyMonkey.com, PollDaddy.com, Zoomerang.com, ask your audience to participate in a short (I mean it!) survey on your topic. Make sure you promise to use the results and reward the participants with at least a copy of the results, and possibly a gift or entry into a drawing for a cool prize. Facebook Polls show the results right on your page encouraging others to vote and share the poll on their pages.

- Research - share important studies about your topic as they are released. Let people know what the latest research is saying about your field. Pull out some of the more interesting subjects as a set up for posting a link to the full article or file.

- Case studies – Do you have some amazing stories of transformation and community impact that you can share with your audience? Make sure to highlight these success stories regularly so people can really connect to your mission and get fired up to support your organization financially and with their many muscle-powered talents – volunteering, spreading your message, representing your organization at events and more

- Share informational articles – Create your own fascinating blog posts or share others that you have found interesting. Make sure they are relevant!

- Step-by-step how to or problem solving guides – Get to the heart of the matter – outline your approach for solving the problems facing the population you serve, get experts in your field to lay out simple strategies for improving health, finding jobs, creating opportunities – whatever topics fit your niche.

- Customer questions – One organization I follow asks a 10PM customer question every day. Their audience consists of teachers and parents, so every day they highlight one question and get hundreds of people to weigh in with suggestions, advice, resources, additional questions and more. This is a great way to make members of your audience into featured heroes and stimulate meaningful conversations about real issues facing your tribe.

- Statistics and facts - It is simply a fact that people gobble up statistics. I love knowing that a chameleon's tongue catches a fly at a higher speed than a jet taking off. I will never need to use that information, but like Cliff Clavin from Cheers, I will never forget it! Thank you to whomever shared that lovely tidbit on Facebook the other day. You can concentrate on more relevant stats, but throw a doozie of a strange one in there every now and then to shake things up and see if people are paying attention.

- Secret Jargon Decoder Ring – Does your topic have a dense curtain of jargon that separates experts from newbies? Help people out by decoding the tech, science, math or theory behind your subject. People will thank you for helping them get smarter on your topic!

- Funnies – There are a lot of funny things circulating around the Internet. When you catch one that fits your audience, please share it! We need more laughter in our days. US Science and Engineering is a great Facebook page to follow for smart, sassy pictures and quotes about nerdy subjects. I love and share their content frequently, and apparently my nerdy friends love them too because they get a lot of play.

- Quotes – This one is a sore spot, because there are so many erroneous quotes floating around the Internet, but if you can verify sources, keep a list of quotes and their attributed sources in circulation on your page.

- Quizzes – Ask people to guess the answer to a regular quiz question. I've used this with great success at a conference where attendees texted in their answers and the results were revealed live. You can also do this on Facebook with poll questions, with plain text or a graphic with the answer and choices. Don't forget to reveal the answer when you promised to reveal it!

- Jokes – Ok, lighten up already! People get tired of your serious issue-related banter and need to know you have another dimension to your personality as an organization. Tell a clean, fun, relevant joke now and then to break the ice crystals forming on your dull and lifeless page.

- Ask for feedback – More than just a simple question, this is an invitation to turn the microscope on your organization and get feedback about your content, your mission, your events, your reputation, your strategy, your volunteer opportunities and more. Don't be afraid to ask how people feel about your organization, and honor responses by thanking them and letting them know you are planning to incorporate their advice as much as you can.

Rich Media Content

Pages that just circulate text quotes on a little robot-posting machine (and you know who you are) are super boring! So spice it up by varying your content. There is so much more to online life than typed tidbits!

Make sure to add at least one of these options to your daily rotation:

- Pictures – The Internet engagement contest will be won by the team with the best pictures. If you are using your own pictures (and you should) please add a watermark with your company's website and logo in a photo editor like Photoshop or one of the many mobile apps that allow you to apply text to pictures like Over or Whim. That way when they are shared and downloaded and shared again, they will always contain a way to get back to your organization. What kinds of pictures should you share?

  - Inspirational quotes with beautiful backgrounds

  - Single tips about your topic with an illustration

  - Live event coverage – any time you attend or host an event, post pictures and tag the people in the pictures

  - Cause awareness/statistics – remember how people love facts and statistics? Well that slick tongued chameleon was staring back at me when I read that fact and it really stuck with me (pun intended).

- New product or service announcements – Share the beauty shot of your new product as a picture, as the background for your page or header image. On Facebook, tag partners or major supporters that you know are in support of your launch (with their permission of course).

- Infographics – If everyone loves facts and statistics, they are even more crazy about infographics which present the facts and stats in beautiful graphical form with charts, graphs and limited explanatory text so that they numbers come alive. Share others' and get your own infographics made to support your cause and watch your sharing go through the roof.

- Sound files - Are you podcasting? Maybe you should be! Podcasts are simply recordings that you can upload to podcasting services. You can record them using a nice microphone on your computer, use your cell phone voice recorder or record and automatically distribute them through an online radio network.

- Music - Are there favorite songs that represent your brand? You can share music from most major online music services. Some prominent charities have sold music compilations to raise funds for many years. Associating your charity brand with music can create powerful connections with your donors.

- Screencasts – Every presentation you give is an opportunity to spread your message even further than the room you are in. Make sure you leverage your slides and/or speech further.

    - Upload your PowerPoint or Keynote presentations to ScreenShare.net with or without an audio soundtrack

    - Record demonstrations of website features or software products using Camtasia or Screenflow (MAC) to introduce your website or record a webinar

- eBooks – Chances are that your audience is searching for your expertise online and would gladly pay for an eBook that gives them that knowledge and supports your organization.

- Offer a free download of an eBook by an expert on your topic in exchange for contact information

- Offer transcripts of a video or speech as a download

- Write a "How To" or advice guide on your topic

- Promote your eBook to your community

- Publish your eBook through Amazon.com or other services

- Videos – Video is the top medium for learning about any subject these days. If you are not at the top of the video results for your key topics, it is time to get out there.

  - What are the top 10-20 questions that people ask about your subject? What should they be asking? Book a half-day session with a good cameraperson shooting interview footage of your organization's experts answering these questions and "drip" your video content out to social networks and video sites over the course of a few weeks.

  - You can also have the camera man record footage of your operations and basic pitch for support to create a 1-3 minute edited "commercial" about your organization

  - Whenever you can, record footage of case studies, testimonials from donors and clients, your events, provide a virtual tour of your offices or facilities and instructional videos that will serve clients and potential clients.

- Events – Whether they are your events, community events or another non-profit's events, you should be documenting and sharing the experience online.

  - Whenever you are having an event, you need to post the event invitation or ticket page everywhere. Facebook events is a handy tool to create awareness of your event, but you need to drive people to a page where they can actually purchase a ticket and you can manage the inventory of tickets and guest lists.

- For ticketing, I recommend Eventbrite.com. You can set up all kinds of packages, including free tickets and promotional code discounts. You pay a processing fee for each paid ticket, but they take care of everything including producing your guest list for checkin. You can also create a public affiliate program, which allows anyone to sign up to promote your event for a commission. This could be a great way to get other non-profits, media companies and others to support your event and sell out your tickets quickly.

- Once your event is over, post event content quickly and tag participants – sharing their photos, videos, testimonials makes the event come alive for those who couldn't make it this year. Seeing the commitment and recognition of their friends should spark a few more volunteers and dollars in the future.

- Getting audience participation – So many ideas have taken off in cause-oriented social media in the past few years. You may have seen causes asking supporters to:

  o   Change their profile pictures

  o   Send suggested statuses, posts, pictures or videos

  o   Answer polls/questions

  o   Share, like or comment on your posts

I encourage you to open up a document and brainstorm 5-10 ideas in each of these categories to form the skeleton of your content plan. For text posts, you can also start to flesh out what you will say and how often you will say it.

Many social networks like Facebook and Twitter will not let you rotate content very frequently. You may need to change up wording and post similar content every few weeks to a month apart.

Remember that not everyone is watching social media all the time, so you should also study the best times to reach your audience. If they are stay-at-home moms, their hours of social media consumption will be different than if they are office workers, for example.

Identify any content that needs to be produced like videos, blog articles or photo enhancements. Delegate the creation of that content to talented team members, volunteers, donors or outsource it to an agency.

> **Bonus Tip:** Set up a Google Alert for your topic keywords and organization name and every day you'll get a special delivery of the latest articles and news stories on your topic that you can share with your audience. You can also visit each of these links and add comments on their stories linking back to one of your destination links. This should drive more content to your sites and help your search engine results.
>
> **Bonus Tip:** User generated content has been all the rage with brand marketers. Have your audience send in their pictures, videos, ideas and more. There are great tools available to moderate contests like Wildfireapp.com. Or you could get all of the submissions directly to your Facebook page, website or email address. Make sure your supporters know that you intend to post the best ones.

Step 5: Choose and Implement Your Update System

Now that you have planned your content calendar, it is time to kick off your campaigns. Think of this in terms of campaigns. Campaigns have a distinct beginning and end, and every piece of communication is woven together into a beautiful fabric – your consistent theme. Generally, campaigns are focused on achieving a specific goal. Go back through your list of messaging ideas and organize them into campaigns – one for each month can work nicely, or perhaps your organization has a reason to be tied to a holiday period or season of the year. In any case, it is good to be organized into a time-boxed campaign calendar tied to goals.

Now you are ready to start posting. You've got some choices here. Either post a little every day, at staggered intervals during the day. This approach helps you look more natural and authentic as you are able to respond to comments quickly and adapt your messaging to the things that are going on in the world and on your pages.

Another option is to find a social media management tool that works best for you and programming the content to release over time. This helps you spend a couple hours a week or month on scheduling posts. You'll still need to log-in daily to manage comments or share other forms of content, but at least your pages will be dynamic and interesting.

I recommend using Send Social Media for your social media management since it is the most powerful tool I've found so far. With this tool, you can:

1. Manage your entire Facebook account, personal and professional pages

2. Manage your Twitter account with enhanced features like autoresponders, following and unfollowing rules

3. Schedule posts to over 30+ social networks

4. View your posts in a calendar

5. View detailed analytics on every post

6. Build a customer database in a unified address book

7. Manage all of your social streams in one unified inbox!

Take advantage of a free 30 day trial of Send Social Media.

Establishing a Consistent Posting and Responding Ritual

The most important thing is to commit to a schedule, a content plan, and a frequency of follow up and stick to them. The ritual that works for me is to spend about 10 minutes at the beginning of the day reading articles on my subjects of interest and posting the good ones. Then I check my emails and social media messages for about 10 minutes. Then I figure out what I'm inspired to say and live post at least one spontaneous item for 5 minutes. Then I add any extra ideas to a post-scheduling tool for 5 minutes.

I check in again at the end of the day, answering people, re-tweeting or reposting good stuff, and adding a life post or noting new ideas in my content scheduler. This takes about 15 minutes at the end of the day. It is a great way to unwind from a long day and stay in touch with people in my area of interest.

Just like email distractions, if you leave social networks open all day, you may never get any work done! You may find that you need to check more frequently or at different times of day when your supporters are most active. Make a plan and a ritual that works for you!

> **Beware!** If you do use a social media management tool to pre-program your content release and something outrageously bad or unbelievably good happens in your industry, you discontinue something you have programmed posts about or some other odd disruption like a major donor leaving, or a flare up of negative comments on one of your posts happens, you must review and delete upcoming comments that would seem "off" at best given the circumstances.

Step 6: Measure and Optimize

Chances are that if you decide to put time, energy and money into your social media strategy, someone on your board or your donors will want to know if those resources were well spent. So it is incredibly important to set yourself up for success by measuring everything you do in social media.

Google Analytics – Measure your website traffic and the achievement of specific goals like completion of a donation process. This helps you understand visits, conversion and completion of donation goals. You can see which pages got the most traffic as well. If you are not techie, ask for help to set this up.

Bit.ly – All of your links are shortened and trackable and in your spreadsheet, right? Now you can go back to Bit.ly and see how many clicks you got on each link and where the traffic came from.

Track Your Audience and Stats on Each Social Network – Each network has their own counting mechanism for determining the size of your audience, and some, like Facebook, provide analytics on how many people engaged with your content.

Go back to your plan armed with these results and determine what you should change in order to improve your results.

Step 7: Empower Your Tribe

Now assuming that you followed the previous steps, you now have a ton of people engaging in your messaging and responding to your requests for support. It is time to ask them what they like, don't like and wish they knew about your subject or your organization.

Can you imagine the new content ideas that will come out of this? This will show your audience that you care about them and make them even more passionate advocates. Provide each of them with a short toolkit – just a few pages – with your key message and supporting facts, as well as suggested posts and links to share with their contacts. Provide special rewards or recognition for those who help you spread the word. There is no telling what a t-shirt or mug will do to motivate a passionate supporter with the right messaging.

Make sure your board and donors are aware of your successes in this area and support you actively with resources and their own special efforts at messaging.

Keep following and emulating the practices of other successful charities, media companies and even for profit businesses in order to find new ideas for content and strategies for engagement. Social media tools are changing everyday, and you will need to be nimble and observant to take advantage of key trends and new capabilities as they arise.

Action Steps:

1. Bookmark this whole section for future reference and work through the steps.

2. Go back through the steps in this chapter and fill your notebook with content ideas and to dos.

3. From there, create a content strategy, lay out your content calendar and brainstorm topics for each theme. Send Social Media is a great tool for programming your social media calendar and tracking results.

4. If you need coaching, consulting or training in this area, visit http://TheCauseBook.com and join our mailing list to receive more resources, videos, webinars and downloadable templates.

Chapter 12: Cross-Channel Marketing Integration

I say luck is when an opportunity comes along, and you're prepared for it.
Denzel Washington

Please make sure you don't spend another dime on traditional marketing without making sure that your messages direct them to engage with your cause on the other platforms where you share content. Remember, you are hosting a virtual "cocktail party" for supporters, and it is only polite to keep inviting more people to join you!

I know that the strong temptation will be to invite them to 15 different social media accounts from one flyer or business card. This is confusing and ineffective. You will end up turning them off and they won't take any action.

Instead, invite them to go to your main "gateway" social networks. Choose 1-3 of whichever networks supports the strongest, most vibrant and active community of your supporters and invite people to join the conversation there. You can always cross-promote to get them to connect with you on other networks from that starting point.

You should also attempt to capture a name, email address and phone number from prospective supporters with traditional marketing. Offer to send them something valuable – a special report, freebie, or a chance to win a prize, if they opt-in to your list. You can integrate a QR code, text messaging instructions or a special website address featuring a video and invitation to join the list.

Text **TheCause**, your name and email address, to **58885** or scan this code to join "The

Cause" Mailing List for more free cause marketing resources!

Your Best Communication Channels

Most non-profits do not spend time thinking about this topic. Their channels are in person meetings, closed-door board meetings, executive committee meetings, fundraising events and direct mail. Some call, some email, a few are starting to use social media. Very few realize the supreme power of building, engaging, retaining and encouraging donations and volunteers from a cohesive list building strategy.

The power of your list is tremendous. Your list is comprised of any emails, phone numbers, addresses or other contact information you have obtained with express permission to contact them about your organization in the future.

Bonus Tip: You rent social media accounts, but you own your "list".

You can communicate with your opt-in list of prospects, donors, volunteers and other supporters any time you want. With social media, you are at the mercy of the social networks' ever changing rules and race to profitability. Case in point: after many brands spent tons of time and money building a Facebook page following, Facebook decided to restrict the reach of each post to just a fraction of the page followers. Now page owners have to pay to promote their posts to the people who already like them.

With your list, you make the rules of engagement, and you are in control. With social media, you are always dealing with whimsy of your landlords who can raise the rent and change the rules any time.

Of course, your list and your use of social media can feed each other, but your primary goal should be to build a solid database of supporters that you can contact in several different ways.

Often times the list is thought of as a donor's list. However, we suggest that you segment your list into several categories:

- Major donors

- Other levels of donors (split this as many times as you need to to track communication and distribute benefits properly by level)

- One time only donors

- Donors more than a year old

- Volunteers

- Press

- Other supporters

When you go to a networking event, seminar or other event, always start a new group or segment of your list. You can write to everyone you meet (once) and invite them to join your main list, invite them to visit your website or watch your videos to learn more about your organization or make a donation.

With every communication, you should strive to collect a little more information:

- Name

- Email

- Permission to email

- Address

- Phone number

- Permission to text

- Social media accounts

- Website

- Employer

- Does the employer offer matching gifts?

Staying in touch with supporters can seem like a full time job! There are so many new and confusing communication channels to cover – people live on their mobile phones and social media – and it can be overwhelming to learn.

There are great tools that make it easy for you to communicate in multiple communication channels with ease! RovingFans.com offers an all in one communication system that lets you instantly send text, email, voicemail messages and social media posts from one convenient website. Another favorite, Instant Customer.com, allows you to create great opt-in tools to build your list, then send email, text, voicemail messages as well as host video, build simple membership sites and more.

Using these tools, it is easy for supporters to sign up on your website, on Facebook, by scanning a QR code or by texting a keyword to a shortcode that we provide when you sign up.

Here are examples of how one of these incredible systems can benefit your organization's communication:

SMS Text Messages

In the past five years, nearly everyone with a cell phone has learned to use text messaging and it is the highest response direct marketing channel out there. No one can resist looking at their phone the second they hear their notification bell ring. Nearly all text messages are read in the first few minutes of receipt. You can use text messaging to send almost any quick short message:

- Send alerts about last-minute "snow day" school closures, cancellations or natural disasters

- Inform supporters of important events, progress, news, and special reports

- Remind subscribers of deadlines, last minute tickets, upcoming volunteer needs

Here are example messages from education settings as examples:

"Please be advised. The University library will be open from 7:00 AM to 11:00 PM during finals week. Take advantage of the extended hours. Good luck, Lions!"

"Don't forget to attend our first rally at Larkin High School @5:00PM! See you all there!"

"Attention students: late tuition payments are due on September 15. Please make your payments at Thompson Hall. Thank you"

Text Contests

People love joining text contests – I have created campaigns like this for dozens of companies (large and small) to use in stadiums, concerts, live events, street festivals, management conferences, tradeshows and more. It can be promoted by signage, in your presentations, announced from the stage, on packaging or promotional items, on staff t-shirts or in your event program.

You can hold a drawing at any event by asking people to text to win a prize. Once you have closed the period for entries, simply pick a random number that has texted in, and text back that they are the winner and how to collect their prize.

Voice Broadcasts

Voice messages are sent directly to subscribers' phones and can give a more personal touch. You can use this feature to announce last-minute event or program changes with a direct and effective voice message.

If you have a celebrity endorser, having them record a short message about your organization and sending it to subscribers can be a real, unexpected thrill! I ran a series of campaigns for a large telecom provider leveraging a celebrity athlete's voice to talk about a promotion and the campaign received an astonishing 40+% response rate!

E-Newsletters

Every organization should be sending emails to their subscribers to inform, educate and inspire them to remain engaged. Share case studies, progress reports, links to your website or annual report, upcoming events, staff profiles, highlight available resources, talk about urgent needs, and fundraising appeals. Adding a video can be a nice touch to personalize the communication.

You can also incorporate your social network buttons into your emails to help them find you on different platforms.

Social Media

Imagine being able to update both Facebook and Twitter instantly with important events and updates. You can post pictures, supporters of the month, big wins, important updates, announcements, achievements, performances, events, and videos instantly.

Using RovingFans.com, add a picture and write "Congratulations to this year's Prom King and Queen – Jane Huckleberry and Matt Harvey!"

This will allow your community to comment and interact with your organization on social media, building a closer community.

Online Sign-up Forms for Building Your List

RovingFans.com makes it easy to set up online sign-up

forms to organize teams and committees with convenient online sign-up pages that are already designed for you. All you do is name and describe the reason for your list and pick a design. Then you get a link that you can share with your contacts in person, via email, text or social media. This makes it easy for volunteers to sign up for events, committees, clubs and special events.

What's a Mobile Keyword?

Have you watched shows like American Idol where they say text a word to a 5- or 6-digit number? And millions of viewers do it? That special word is called a keyword and it helps people join your list just by texting that word to a special code called a "Shortcode" which is like a short phone number for your texting program.

You can use this to get people to join your lists at events, meetings and on signage around town or on social media.

It always helps to provide incentives to join. For example, invite supporters at live events to text in the keyword for a chance to win organization gear or gift cards.

To try this out, and to join our list for more free cause marketing resources and special offers, text the keyword **TheCause**, your name and your email to **58885**.

Send a text message to join "The Cause" list.

Mobile Voting

Supporters can participate in entertaining quizzes or partake in voting during assemblies to give immediate feedback! This feature is great for finding out more about what supporters want so you can improve your organization's offerings.

For example, "Which International Week performance did you like the best? 1) Traditional drum circle 2) Cultural history play 3) Polynesian dance"

Text-to-Screen

Text to screen is an engaging way for live event attendees alike to text questions and comments to a public display screen for all to see. This is perfect for sporting events, concerts, plays, assemblies, galas, dances, seminars, and more!

Don't forget Alumni and Past Supporters!

Active alumni can translate into donations, opportunities for current students, and positive promotion of your school name. Alumni can also register their names, mobile numbers, email, and other custom data to stay in the loop.

5 Quick List Building Strategies

There are so many ways to build your list rapidly. Here are just a few to get you started:

1.   *Get opt-ins at events* – any time you are speaking, tell the crowd that they can get your slides, a free e-Book or another valuable gift by texting your keyword to a shortcode.

2.   *Having an opt-in box on your website* – Alert your webmaster to add a box to capture name, email, mobile phone number and permission to recontact asap. There should be a good incentive to join the list like the free e-Book, videos or a gift and it should be featured prominently on your site, ideally in the upper right hand side of the screen according to many tests.

3.   *Have an opt-in page or form linked from social networks* – The link that you put in your social media profiles can go right to your opt-in page.

4.   *Have a vote* – publicize a vote or poll on your Facebook pages or events. Everyone who votes will join your list.

5.   *Text*-to-Screen – at your next event, have a Text-to-Screen experience. Everyone who texts to see their message on the screen will be opting in for more information from you.

Action Item:

1.   Try one or both of these recommended systems to improve your communication with your donors, volunteers, and supporters. If you need training or assistance in setting up campaigns, please contact us through **DDx Media**.

- RovingFans.com offers an exclusive 10-day free trial and excellent training videos. It lets you manage your opt-in forms, mobile keywords, and contact lists for email, text, voice calls, social media posts, mobile voting, text-to-screen and much much more. It is a great tool for supporter engagement.

- Instant Customer offers a 21-day trial for just $1 and offers multi-channel communication campaign management tools including email, text, voice calls, QR codes, direct mail webpage builders, integrated payment options and preformatted templates for campaigns.

Chapter 13: Mobile Applications

People of accomplishment rarely sat back & let things happen to them. They went out and happened to things.
Leonardo Da Vinci

Chances are you have been convinced to create a website for your organization in the past ten or so years. A website is a great destination to send your supporters and educate them on your mission, collect donations and share news.

However, a lot has changed in the past few years. We are in the midst of a communication revolution with the rapid explosion of mobile phones and tablets. People are using mobile apps as much as they are watching TV or using a desktop computer.

Chances are even stronger that your website is not keeping up with this trend. Are you on the app bandwagon yet? Here are eight reasons you should be:

Reason 1: Your Website Looks Awful on a Mobile Phone

Really. I'm serious. Check it out right now. Open a web browser on your mobile phone and then pull up your website. Can you read that thing? Do you know what to do? Are you pinching and zooming all over to try to figure it out? Are there big missing chunks because many mobile phones don't handle Flash?

When you arrived at this website, you probably took the time to look around and examine what you could do. The big problem is that while you actually care enough about your website to try to make sense of it on a phone, your prospects who find you on a phone won't have the patience.

They'll be moving on to a site that is optimized for mobile or to an app from a organization that provides them with a convenient, easy to use experience on a mobile website or an app.

Reason #2: Attention, Please! Your Prospects Spend 4+ Hours a Day on a Smartphone

Nothing holds a prospect's attention like their personal, beloved mobile phone. Nothing. People use mobile phones while doing just about anything – watching TV, riding in a car (hopefully not driving, people!), sitting on a train, and let's be honest, even going to the bathroom. This gadget is absolutely captivating and you want your brand to be found and enjoyed on mobile phones and tablets.

Reason #3 With an App, Your Brand is Always Accessible

An app is basically a small software program that is downloaded and installed on a customer's phone. A great deal of content can be included in that installation package, so a customer can open the app and see your brand and content without being connected to the internet via 3G or Wi-Fi. Of course, most people get the jitters when they are not connected, but since they'll be able to find your branded app and be entertained by it during their downtime, you'll be giving them a great experience.

Reason #4: Apps Are Engaging

With an app, you can put all of the tools for connecting with your brand in one easy to navigate package, providing better, quicker, more responsive customer service, a slick, easy to use, downright pleasant buying experience, and fun content or experiences like checking-in at your location to earn coupons or rewards.

Reason #5: Apps Help You Reward Loyal Supporters

We love creating mobile rewards programs for organizations that want to give treats to customers that come in to volunteer or give often.

You know those frequent buyer punchcards taking up space in your wallet or on your bathroom counter top? Yeah, we forget them at home on our bathroom counters too and then we get mad. Sometimes we don't go in to make a purchase because we don't have our card. We don't want that to happen with your volunteers!

With mobile rewards built into an app, everyone is practically guaranteed to have their card with them, because it is built into an app on their phone! You can track their volunteer hours and reward them when they reach a certain milestone.

Reason #6: Apps Can Notify Customers of New Content

The biggest challenge with apps is keeping people coming back. There are great ways of waking customers up and reminding them of the value, fun and usefulness of your app, including sending push notifications about breaking news or special limited time offers or even doing an update of the app. It's great to see spikes in usage after a notification or an update because you know your customers are getting reminded about your organization and invited to take actions within your app.

Reason #7: Apps Are Permanent Real Estate on Your Customer's Phone

What if you could put your customer database and a cash register in your customer's pocket? With an app, you can get customers to provide their contact information, permission to contact them with email or text messages, and even a full mobile shopping or menu ordering experience right in their phone!

The best part is, once it is installed, it stays installed unless it is deleted. This gives your brand a permanent icon and listing on the phone menu, putting your most vital customer retention and sales tools in their hand at all times.

Reason #8: You Can Collect Contact Information and Donations with an App

Your app can be a lead generation tool and convert interested contacts into donors. While Apple has some strict regulations about accepting donations in an app, you can work around this issue. We can incorporate your opt-in page and collect donations in a number of creative ways to help you improve your financial opportunities.

Apps are great for engagement with donors at events as well. Ask the audience to take out their phones and join your list or make a donation by downloading your app!

Action Item:

1. Are you excited to get started on an app? Custom developed mobile apps are very expensive to produce, but Amaze Mobile Solutions, offers extremely reasonable and high quality apps for non-profits. Learn more and request a free mobile app demo at AmazeMobile.com. Mention "TheCauseBook" for a special offer.

2. Download "The Cause – Resources for Non-Profit Leaders and Social Entrepreneurs" app for extra free resources! Search your app store or scan the QR code below.

Chapter 14: Other Online Fundraising Opportunities

Opportunity is missed by most people because it is dressed in overalls and looks like work.
Thomas A. Edison

Grants

There are tons of online grant applications in nearly every field that are available for those who apply. The gifts may be in the form of money, hardware, service hours or software. For edRover, we won grants from Compute.org and Netsuite.org. It just takes patience and persistence, along with the terrific storytelling pitch you have developed.

One incredible opportunity is to sign up for free advertising grants from Google. Read through the current program details and join here - http://www.google.com/nonprofits/.

Search the Internet for the word grant and a generic description of your program to see what opportunities may pop up for your organization, then take massive action!

When you are working with an online grant application, make sure you fill out the questions in a Word or Pages document first, then transfer your answers into the form by cutting and pasting. Some forms expire after 5 minutes without a submission, and you don't want to lose all of our information. It is also good to keep a record of what you've submitted for your records and to speed up the process for future grant applications.

Sometimes it takes a few months to get a response, but keep connecting with the organization to check on status and hopefully you will have a great new supporter soon.

Paid Advertising

If you do have a budget for advertising, and you'd like to get the word out faster, there are many places you can run a highly targeted paid advertising campaign:

- Facebook friends of friends campaign – targets people who are friends of those who already like you

- YouTube

- Google

- Slideshare

- LinkedIn

Before setting up a campaign, consider your audience and always check for any special program or promotion for non-profits for which you may be eligible to apply.

If you are promoting your app, the best places to advertise on a limited budget are:

- AdWhirrl - consolidates access to multiple mobile ad networks

- Flurry – App Circle lets you earn money from advertising in your app and shows your app to others in similar apps

- Facebook mobile app ads

Please contact us at DDx-Media.com if you need help with paid media campaigns.

Awards

Applying for or pitching for awards should be much easier now that you know how to tell your story in words, pictures and videos. You may find awards opportunities in your area, from industry newsletters or at trade shows.

I have found great financial success and publicity from entering and winning awards for my cause fundraising platform, edRover.com. We won major awards from AT&T, Microsoft, ComputerWorld and StayClassy.org.

I've also coached organizations pitching in the Los Angeles Social Venture Partners Fast Pitch Competition. There are organizations and events like this all across the country and they are a great way to increase visibility for your work in the community.

Be on the look out for opportunities to apply, and never miss a deadline! You are just one pitch away from greatness.

Put all of the communication and storytelling tips that you have learned in this book by applying for an awards program today!

I would love for you to take a break from the book and watch some of the pitches from the candidates that we have coached.

Go to http://bit.ly/LASVPFastpitch to see the finalist pitches in action.

Incredible stories and impact messages, right? All of these people started out right where you are, but without this book and recommended tools to help them. Just think about where you can go with your storytelling!

Online Contests

In the past few years, online contests have been all the rage. One of my organizations was involved in the Chase/Living Social $250,000 contest in 2012 and a $25,000 Pepsi contest in 2011. If you are lucky enough to be in a social voting contest, be prepared to mobilize an intensely large and loyal army of daily voters. Carefully scouring the rules on day one to determine what is allowable and disallowed will help you quickly build your strategy.

For some contests, you are allowed multiple votes, so working with others in voting coalitions has seemed to work. Often you will find Facebook groups dedicated to people helping each other with these contests. Even if you don't win, it can be good for your brand exposure and sending traffic to your website.

Some of the downsides? They are a severe time and energy drain. If your standing start to decrease, people get discouraged and get tired of hearing you ask to vote incessantly. Groups with large, loyal social networks have unbeatable voting power, so it is far from a sure thing.

The lesson? Follow the steps in this book to build your loyal following for just this situation! When a major online contest comes up, you want to be in a strong position to mobilize your audience to support your cause.

Social Donations and Crowdfunding for Charities

Another major trend in the past few years is the rise of crowdfunding sites. Once you have built your audience, have refined your pitch and built your compelling support packages, you may want to try your hand at building a page on one of the crowdfunding sites and promoting it to boost your contribution.

Recent famous examples of successful crowdfunding campaign was the "Inocente" documentary that went on to win an Oscar in 2013 (Kickstarter) and the Kony 2012 campaign that generated 100+ million video views and millions in donations (StayClassy).

There are over 450 crowdfunding sites, and that number is growing fast. Crowdfunding has actually been around for a long time in the form of getting small sponsorships from friends and family for races, walk-a-thons, and other generally athletic pursuits. With crowdfunding websites, the same asking friends and family to support a project or cause can be extended to the friends and family of your friends and family easily through social sharing.

There are two main crowdfunding models – single-tier and multi-tier. Single tier sites help you set up a main organization page and sharing it with your supporters who can share your main page with their friends and family. Multi-tier crowdfunding sites allow each of your customers to set up a page with their own personal story about why they support your cause. They use your approved content, but add their personal touch which can greatly increase the effectiveness of their appeal. Of course, all funds donated go to your organization in either scenario (minus the processing fees).

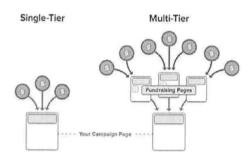

Source: StayClassy.org

Each of the sites has a slightly different business model – some have monthly fees, some charge a larger percentage of all transactions. All will charge a per transaction fee to cover credit card processing. Some require you to make the appeal project-based, and some allow you to have an open ended campaign. Some focus on an "all or nothing" policy which can increase urgency, but if you don't reach your campaign goal in time, you are out of luck and get nothing for your hard work. Your donors are refunded in that scenario. Some allow you to have team fundraising pages or tie your campaign to a physical event like a race, walk or benefit concert.

Shop around at different sites to find one that works best for you. You should be able to find a great crowdfunding site that will help you build a super social media friendly, credit card accepting donation page through which you can share your new story and build support. We are fans of StayClassy.org if you are looking for a good place to start.

The same social media engagement techniques apply – you will need to stay very active to promote your campaign. It is good to set a deadline for support to create urgency and to prevent burnout among your supporters.

When you do well with any of these activities, they look great to other supporters, can help your organization financially, and if you've been doing the exercises in the book, you are ready to win!

Social Shopping for Your Cause

If you'd like to equip your supporters with an online and mobile shopping and eGiftcard portal that gives back substantial rebates to your school, check out edRover.com.

Action Item:

1. Go to TheCauseBook.com and join our community where we share great current resources about online fundraising tools, contests, and awards opportunities.

2. Make a commitment to yourself in your notebook to find and apply for at least 4 of these opportunities this year.

3. Check out edRover.com and start earning money for your school.

4. If you represent a charity that would like to take advantage of the platform, email ed@edRover.com.

Chapter 15: Leveraging Community Resources

The community stagnates without the impulse of the individual.
The impulse dies away without the sympathy of the community.
William James

You already have a network of resources that you've been cultivating for years, including your local media contacts, local businesses, vendors, alumni, previous donors, friends and family.

Make sure that you start your explosive communication initiative by reaching out to them! It is time to put all of your hard work, soul searching, donor persona profiling, emotional but rational storytelling to the test with the people who know and love you best. Your first job will be to share your story and the goals of your campaign, and to enlist them as active ambassadors for your story.

Please share the techniques and tools you've learned by reading this book to help them put words and images to their personal story of connection to your cause so that when they make the case for support, it is equally as impactful. Of course, handing them a copy of this book may be the best inspiration of all!

Action Items:

1. Inspire and Activate Your Nonprofit Board

    a. Make sure your board is educated about your goals and the new strategies you've learned

    b. Pass around this book or provide them with copies so that they can read the recommendations for themselves

    c.   Once your plan is outlined, ask for their support and the initial resources you need to start an effective digital media outreach campaign

    d.   Make sure the Board Members get social media accounts and connect to you too. When they see it working, they will be more than believers. You are giving them the tools to be social media advocates too!

    e.   Report back frequently – share your digital media successes, challenges, adjusted plans and more. This is a continuous learning and growth process!

    f.   Hold them accountable for actively sharing your messages!

2.   Enroll and Activate Donors, Friends & Family

    a.   Ask your previous donors, friends, family, clients and volunteers to connect with your organization on social media and share their personal stories with you

    b.   They would be great initial interview subjects and testimonials. Invite them over for a filming day!

    c.   Get feedback on your plan before you send it out

3.   Send out your sponsorship package to local media contacts

    a.   Get them on board as media sponsors (trading exposure for press)

    b.   Ask for their help in promoting your new efforts

    c.   Connect with their fans on their social media accounts

    d.   Offer to be a subject matter expert in future interviews on your subject

4.   Engage your local business owners and vendors

a. Share your sponsorship kit with them and ask them to get involved

b. Thank their business on social media and your list communication as a form of recognition for donations and other forms of support

c. Ask them to post about your organization, including your social media pages to build your following rapidly

Chapter 16: This Is Your Time

The time is always right to do what is right.
Martin Luther King Jr.

There is no denying it. You are working in the non-profit sector or as a social entrepreneur at a great time. Cause is hot.

And there are so many free and low cost ways of spreading your unique and compelling story.

According to the IEG Sponsorship Report, cause sponsorship is predicted to reach $1.78 billion in 2013, a projected increase of 4.8% over 2012.

Your organization can rally supporters with a clear message, compelling offering and consistent donor engagement strategy. I hope you take the opportunity to apply what you have learned to make an enormous difference in the course of your organization's history.

Action Items:

1. Get fired up about your personal mission and tell your compelling and authentic story

2. Make sure you have a solid strategic plan enhanced with everything you've learned here.

3. Perfect your pitch by using it frequently

4. Prepare and distribute your sponsorship proposals to win amazing support for your organization

5. Set the social media world on fire with your awesome content

6. Win some great contests and awards!

7. Get out there and make a tremendous impact!

Please stay in touch and share your success stories, questions and suggestions by joining our list at TheCauseBook.com.

About the Author

Tania is the founder and CEO of DDx Media, an award-winning mobile marketer, an entrepreneur, speaker, consultant, a mother of three, and adjunct professor at the University of Southern California. Her ability to bring real world experience and technical aptitude for the mobile experience, her penchant for entrepreneurship and her passion for learning led to comments such as "inspirational" and "super cool" by the students.

"There's security in staying with what you know. But there are a lot of other interesting pursuits out there. Take a chance and do something you've always dreamed of doing." In 2010, Tania took her own advice and took the plunge – leaving her corporate career to pursue her dream of doing something that would help the world. It was from this idea that she founded DDx Media. The company's first initiative was developing edRover, a mobile app that helps families to direct donations from online and instant mobile giftcard purchases to a school of their choice.

edRover was recognized by AT&T as the Best Application of 2011 in the category of Social Good. Impressed by the edRover concept and Tania's contest pitch, AT&T asked her to join the AT&T Developers' Advisory Council. She also won Microsoft Fastpitch Competition and was among a few developers selected to attend Microsoft Mobile Acceleration Week.

Prior to striking out on her own with DDx, Tania was a key member of an international marketing agency, developing cutting edge digital and experiential marketing campaigns for an impressive roster of clients. These clients included AT&T, JCPenney, GameStop, Brinkers (Chili's), Nintendo, Nokia, RIM, LG, State Farm, Kimberly-Clark, Frito-Lay, the San Diego Chargers, the Dallas Cowboys, the New York Yankees, the San Francisco Giants, and the San Antonio Spurs.

Tania was also a founding member of MasterCard Worldwide's Information Products and Services team, which still yields the company over $50 annually million in revenue. She led MasterCard's mobile marketing, loyalty, and commerce initiatives, including business development with major banks, mobile network operators, handset manufacturers and mobile wallet suppliers.

Tania is recognized as an international and U.S. patent holder for her work to identify behavioral patterns in purchasing data and predicting more profitable cross-marketing opportunities. She was a key member of the Corporate Strategy team leading up to the historic IPO of MasterCard Worldwide.

When Tania is not teaching or working on her entrepreneurial ventures she is planning her next trip. Her love of travel is related to her interest in education issues, she explained. "Education is about taking your family on an interesting adventure, experiencing life. Sometimes the best part is going on a drive and popping into the places you find along the way."

Tania lives in Northern Los Angeles County with a bunch of boys: her devoted and supportive husband Will, three amazing sons and her dog, Danny.

Tania's personal mission is to inspire others to truly live, give and serve by telling THEIR authentic story.

What is your mission?

Work With DDx Media, Inc.

DDx Media is a digital marketing agency with a heart of gold. We love helping socially conscious businesses get the word out about their mission and make a bigger difference. Find us at DDx-Media.com and contact us if you need help with any of the following services:

- Speaking Engagements

- edRover – Social Shopping and eGiftcard Fundraising and White Label Platform Licensing

- RovingFans.com - All-in-One Messaging Tools

- Amaze Mobile Solutions – Easy, Affordable Mobile Applications for iPhone, iPad, Android and HTML5 Mobile Websites

- Business Coaching & Consulting

- Corporate Training Sessions

- Book a Speaking Engagement with Tania Mulry

- Branding and Messaging Strategy Development

- Mobile App Idea & Product Development Coaching

- Websites & Mobile Websites

- Custom Mobile Applications for iOS, Android, Windows, Blackberry, Kindle, and more

- App Store Optimization and Mobile Media

- Social Media Set-Up & Strategy

- Merchant Accounts

Free Bonus Resources:
To thank you for all that you do to make the world a better place, we've created special bonuses for you at our website. Visit TheCauseBook.com or scan this code with a QR Code reader on your phone:

Please Leave Us a Review on Amazon.com
If you have found this book useful, the best way to help us help other cause leaders find this resource is to review our book on Amazon.com here:

http://bit.ly/TheCauseMulry

Thank You!

DDx Media, Inc.
25876 The Old Road, #65
Stevenson Ranch, CA 91381
800-838-5648
DDx-Media.com

3710142R00076

Printed in Great Britain
by Amazon.co.uk, Ltd.,
Marston Gate.